D0909229

JOHN DRYDEN

D R Y D E N

Poetry & Prose

With Essays by
CONGREVE, JOHNSON, SCOTT
and others

With an Introduction and Notes by
DAVID NICHOL SMITH

OXFORD

AT THE CLARENDON PRESS

Oxford University Press, Amen House, London E.C. 4

GLASGOW NEW YORK TORONTO MELBOURNE WELLINGTON
BOMBAY CALCUTTA MADRAS KARACHI CAPE TOWN IBADAN

Geoffrey Cumberlege, Publisher to the University

FIRST PUBLISHED 1925
REPRINTED WITH CORRECTIONS 1946, 1951, 1955

PRINTED IN GREAT BRITAIN

CONTENTS

THE frontispiece is from the portrait of Dryden
by an unknown painter presented to the University
of Oxford by George Clarke in 1732, and now in the
Bodleian Library

INTRODUCTION

WHEN we read the works of Dryden, we make a study of his age. Most of his longer poems were inspired by political or religious controversy, and were intended to have an immediate influence on public opinion. Other poems celebrate national events, or were written to decorate an occasion, or were suggested by his friendships. He finds his subjects anywhere in the life that is being lived around him. Even when he goes back to other times and translates Virgil or modernizes Chaucer, he has always in mind what his age seemed to him to require. Something of a recluse in private life, at least a man who took an awkward part in conversation and shone only in chosen company, he was nothing of a recluse in his writings. He speaks to his contemporaries, or for them, on the things about which they are thinking. And he speaks in a manner which was familiar to them, and was novel only in its brilliance. He did not, in Coleridge's phrase, create the taste by which he was to be relished or teach the art by which he was to be seen. He never thought of having to wait to be understood; he meant every word of his to be appreciated at its proper value on the day of publication; his controversial poems, and indeed all his occasional poems, would have failed in so far as they were difficult or strange. What he did was to lead the taste of the time in the direction in which it was already going. The range of his work is remarkable. As poet, he writes satires and epistles, odes and songs, prologues and epilogues, elegies, tales, and translations, poems descriptive, argumentative, or didactic; as dramatist, he writes comedies, tragedies, heroic dramas, and operas; as critic, he reviews all the questions in the

art of letters that were at issue in his day, and gives his
estimate of the greatest poets ; as prose-writer he is master
of a style which is equally adaptable to the commonplaces
of exposition, the cut and thrust of controversy, and the
intimacies of conviction.   In every kind of work that he
took in hand he showed his competence ; in almost every
kind he excelled.   His serious rivals were only in the drama.
He admitted that his genius never much inclined him to the
stage, and that he had been outdone by some of his contemporaries in comedy.   As a poet, and a critic, his
pre-eminence was unquestioned.

His early work showed little promise.   The first poem in
which we catch the note of his mature verse is his *Stanzas
on the Death of Cromwell*.   We catch it oftener in his
couplets on the Restoration.   But

> Great Dryden did not early great appear,
> Faintly distinguished in his thirtieth year.[1]

Many years had to pass before he became ' great '.   He
continued to hesitate between the couplet and the ' stanza
of four in alternate rhyme ', and chose this stanza for his
Annus Mirabilis, a poem which has memorable passages,
but gains by being read in extract.   The only great work
that he produced before his fortieth year is his prose essay
Of Dramatic Poesy.   Thereafter, for a dozen years, his
growing energies were devoted to the drama, and the drama
solved for him his metrical problem.   Even the friendliest
criticism finds many faults in his plays, and especially in
his rhymed plays (though they have merits which are often
ignored), but it was in his plays that he learned how to
write the heroic couplet.   When in 1681 [2] he turned to satire
he had perfected his instrument, and could use it with the

[1] Laurence Ensden, in Verses addressed to Lord Halifax, 1709 ;
quoted by Malone in his ' Life of Dryden ', *Prose Works of Dryden*,
1800, vol. i, p. 50.

[2] Or a little earlier : see note on *MacFlecknoe*, p. 188.

confidence of a master. *Absalom and Achitophel* is his first great poem, and he wrote it when he was fifty. With it begins the period of his acknowledged supremacy, which each new poem made more secure. His strength never failed. He writes new kinds of poems, and in new metres ; during all this period of roughly twenty years he welcomes new subjects on which to exercise his skill. The range of his powers was not fully exhibited till he had reached a time of life when most other poets have declined into a settled manner. His very last book, his *Fables*, was an experiment ; he was then in his seventieth year, and he wrote it with the zest of youth. ' A cripple in my limbs, but what decays are in my mind the reader must determine', he says of himself ; and he continues, ' I think myself as vigorous as ever in the faculties of my soul, excepting only my memory, which is not impaired to any great degree; and if I lose not more of it, I have no great reason to complain. What judgement I had increases rather than diminishes ; and thoughts, such as they are, come crowding in so fast upon me, that my only difficulty is to choose or to reject, to run them into verse, or to give them the other harmony of prose.' [1] Dryden's development was unusually protracted, but it never ceased. He never felt that his real work had been done but was always pressing on to something new ; and at no time of his life do we have this sense of movement in his art more clearly than in the three final years of *Alexander's Feast*, *The Secular Masque*, and the *Fables*.

He always thought of his times as a period of reconstruction and adjustment, and habitually spoke of them as the ' new age '. The nation was settling down to more or less stable habits of thought and life after the upheaval of the middle of the century. In politics, its great task was the adjustment of the constitution to the new conditions. In

[1] See p. 163.

literature, its aims were in many ways similar. What was best in the old tradition was to be adapted to the new taste. The men of the Restoration looked back to the Elizabethans much as the younger men of to-day look back to the Victorians. They never disguised their pride in the genius of Shakespeare, or in the learning and judgement of Ben Jonson. No greater eulogy of Shakespeare has ever been written than Dryden's. But times had changed, and men had changed with them, and Elizabethan wit and language and methods were out of date.

> Wit 's now arrived to a more high degree,
> Our native language more refined and free ;
> Our ladies and our men now speak more wit
> In conversation than those poets writ.

So said Dryden in an early epilogue.[1] Another of his early statements, even more surprising to the modern reader, is that ' the sweetness of English verse was never understood by our fathers '—one of whom was Spenser. As a criticism of the Elizabethans it is negligible, but it shows how Dryden set out in the belief that the new poetry had broken with the old ; and it ought to be read in its context, for Dryden is always ready to explain any opinion that he advances (and, it should be added, to withdraw it when he thinks it should not be maintained). In the interval since the Elizabethans our poetry, he says, has been ' improved ', and we have been shown how to carry on the good work : we have ' to mould our thoughts into easy and significant words ; to retrench the superfluities of expression, and to make our rhyme so properly a part of the verse, that it should never mislead the sense, but itself be led and governed by it '.[2] This is, at the least, an excellent statement of the new ideals in verse, and of his own aims.

His hopes for the new age were never fully realized. We

[1] To the *Conquest of Granada*, 1670.
[2] See p. 149.

continually get the impression that he thought of himself
as fighting the battle single-handed, or with too few allies.
It may be that Dryden would not readily bear a rival near
his throne. The men whom he encouraged, and encouraged
with a liberality which they were proud to remember and
to record, were much younger than himself. But the sense
of disappointment is unmistakable. Late in life he
confessed that the new age, with all its promise, and despite
the advantages of what seemed to him to be its better
taste, had not equalled the Elizabethan :

> Our age was cultivated thus at length ;
> But what we gained in skill we lost in strength ;
> Our builders were with want of genius curst ;
> The second temple was not like the first.[1]

Later still, in probably his very last verses, which were
written to bring in the new century, he rejoices that the
new age of his youth, now an old age, is over and done with :

> Tis well an Old Age is out,
> And time to begin a New.[2]

This is more than the commonplace expectation of the
good things a new century is to bring.

If he was disappointed in his age, he never thought
lightly of the part which he had to play in it. A Roman
Catholic since the reign of James II, he had lost the laureateship at the Revolution and could meet with no favour from
William III, but when his health was failing some of his
friends in the government wished to recognize his services
and to ease his continuous struggle against poverty. What
was proposed is not known, and what information we have
is derived from one of his letters. ' The court,' he says,
' rather speaks kindly of me than does anything for me,
though they promise largely. . . . If they will consider me

---

[1] *To Mr. Congreve*, ll. 11–14, p. 110.
[2] *The Secular Masque*, p. 142.

as a man who has done my best to improve the language, and especially the poetry, and will be content with my acquiescence under the present government, and forbearing satire on it, that I can promise, because I can perform it.' [1] Even in the intimacy of a private letter he bases his claims to reward not on any works in particular, but on his continuous endeavour to improve English poetry. That was his service to the nation. The poets and critics of the eighteenth century who claimed kinship with him were of the same opinion. As a rule what they seem to think of first is not the excellence of separate poems but his mastery of verse in general. Pope confessed that he had learned versification wholly from Dryden's works. Gray maintained that 'if there was any excellence in his own numbers, he had learned it wholly from that great poet'. Johnson said that he 'tuned the numbers of English poetry' and attributed to him 'the improvement, perhaps the completion of our metre'.

We cannot attribute this to him now. But the greatness of the metrical achievements of the nineteenth century cannot obscure the greatness of Dryden's. Whatever verse he employs it has a music which at once proclaims the writer. There are some poets—but not many—who give us short passages which might be by Pope ; but once we have caught the note of Dryden's verse we do not mistake another's heroic couplets for his. He established these couplets as one of the chief forms of modern poetry, and he still remains their most individual writer. His have a lift and a swell which carry the reader forward in continual expectation,—which often carried Dryden himself beyond the strict limits of the metre ; and though in his laxer moments he tended to use the triplet and the alexandrine too frequently, and occasionally even the line of fourteen

[1] Letter to Mrs. Steward, 7 November 1699, *Works*, ed. Scott and Saintsbury, xviii, pp. 160–1.

syllables, at his best he won by them conclusive and characteristic effects. The heroic couplet has different movements in the hands of its great masters. For the slow and massive movement we have to go to Johnson ; his finest verse refuses to be read quickly. In no other writer is the movement so rapid as in Dryden. He swings along in exuberant vigour and careless ease.

He was equally at his ease in other forms, whether blank verse, the ode, or the lyric. In his *All for Love* he wrote as good dramatic blank verse as has been written since the Elizabethans. He gave new harmonies to the ode which Cowley had introduced in mistaken imitation of Pindar— the ode which allows each stanza to be a law unto itself. The applause which greeted *Alexander's Feast* continued undiminished till the time of Scott, and though subsequent criticism has objected that its beauties belong rather to rhetoric than to poetry, the skill with which its various metrical effects are produced, and co-ordinated, cannot be denied. He sounds a deeper note in the *Ode on the Death of Mrs. Anne Killigrew* ; it is inferior in structure to both the St. Cecilia Odes, but it makes a more intimate appeal than either of them, for they suffer in this respect from having been written to be set to music. He takes an Horatian ode on the fickleness of Fortune and tries the experiment of transposing it into the Pindaric manner, which suited better with the ' vehemence ' of his temper ; and what begins as a paraphrase becomes an original poem, in which his own feelings are given perfect metrical expression. His songs are of many kinds. They are often trivial, but the best of them have a delicacy and spontaneity which make us regret that he did not take his lyrical gifts more seriously. One metre was apparently as easy to him as another. Always an experimenter, he anticipates measures and cadences that we associate with the nineteenth century ; at other times, he recalls the early

Carolines. Nothing can show better than even a small collection of his lyrics—such as is given in this volume—that Dryden lived in an age of transition ; and on the whole it is the note of what is coming rather than the note of what is passing that we hear most clearly.

He raised the art of satire to the plane which it occupies in the literature of Rome. Of all who preceded him in English, it has to be said, in the words which he used about the youngest of them, that their wit shone ' through the harsh cadence of a rugged line '.[1] Some of them could not but be rough ; others were purposely rough, as if they thought that a coarse and blunt weapon would make the uglier wound. By the time that Dryden came to write his satires he could not go back on the long training which he had received in the drama, and even when he professes to use ' unpolished, rugged verse ',[2] it says, perhaps in an offhand manner, but precisely, what he means it to say. His command of his weapon accounts in part for the new temper which he introduced into English satire. The nicest and most delicate touches, he tells us, consist in fine raillery. ' How easy is it to call rogue and villain, and that wittily ! But how hard to make a man appear a fool, a blockhead, or a knave, without using any of those opprobrious terms ! To spare the grossness of the names, and to do the thing yet more severely, is to draw a full face, and to make the nose and cheeks stand out, and yet not to employ any depth of shadowing. This is the mystery of that noble trade, which yet no master can teach to his apprentice.'[3] None of Dryden's many critics has helped us to a fuller appreciation of his aim and his accomplishment as a satirist than Dryden himself.

He tells us that he thought the character of Zimri in *Absalom and Achitophel* worth the whole poem. We would

[1] *To the Memory of Mr. Oldham*, l. 16, p. 91.
[2] *Religio Laici*, l. 453, p. 90.   [3] See p. 158.

rather say that it is the greatest part of our greatest satire. He had failed in the drama because his characters were not sufficiently individualized; sometimes, it has to be admitted, they were little more than talking or rhyming abstractions. In his *Absalom and Achitophel* he draws real men. If the portraits have the element of caricature that satire demands, the accentuating of some features to the neglect of others, they are none the less life-like. Side by side with them are the friendly portraits, which are excellent in their slighter style. Together they make *Absalom and Achitophel* one of the great national portrait galleries in English poetry, the richest that we have had since Chaucer wrote his Prologue.

In his *Fables* he took Chaucer as his chief model, and there he is at his best, not when he modernizes Chaucer, but when he chooses a story from Boccaccio's *Decameron* and treats it much as Chaucer might have done. Since Chaucer, no better short stories had been told in English verse than Dryden's *Theodore and Honoria* and *Cymon and Iphigenia*. Have any been told better since ? Wordsworth, who was not a favourable critic, thought these tales ' the most poetical of his poems '.[1]

To appreciate Dryden's greatness as a critic, it is sufficient to read what he says of Shakespeare in one of his first essays, and of Chaucer in the last.[2]

We cannot easily point to another author who has shown as great adaptability in so large a number of subjects and

---

[1] Letter to Scott, 7 November 1805, printed in Lockhart's *Life of Scott*, ed. 1839, vol. ii, pp. 287–9.

[2] ' The criticism of Dryden ', said Johnson, ' is the criticism of a poet ; not a dull collection of theorems, nor a rude detection of faults, which perhaps the censor was not able to have committed ; but a gay and vigorous dissertation, where delight is mingled with instruction, and where the author proves his right of judgement by his power of performance.' This follows immediately after the paragraph which ends on p. 5, l. 4.

styles. It is true that he is hasty, and often falls below his promise, for he was a master of the happy opening. A selection chosen only from the first lines of his poems, such as *Religio Laici*, *MacFlecknoe*, the Killigrew Ode, *The Hind and the Panther*, and the translation of the tenth satire of Juvenal, would give a fair idea of his powers. It was not his habit to work up to great passages, but rather to give us his good things as they came to him ; and they came as frequently at once as later. If after a brilliant beginning he trips and stumbles on what he calls a ' flat ', he always forces us onwards in expectation of the happy passage that is bound to follow. We think of him as a great craftsman who exercises his craft with careless confidence and unflagging zest. But the impression that remains with us most strongly is that we have been in the company of a mind of rare vigour, sometimes impetuous, and always ready and undaunted. There are many poets who seem to have written to the top of their capacity. When we understand Dryden we say that he was greater than any of his works.

DRYDEN'S LIFE

1631. John Dryden born at Aldwinckle, Northamptonshire, August 9.

164?–50. At Westminster School, under Dr. Busby.

1650–4. At Trinity College, Cambridge : B.A. 1654.

1659. *Stanzas on the Death of Cromwell* : see p. 180.

1660. The Restoration ; Charles II enters London May 29.
(June) *Astraea Redux*.

1663. *The Wild Gallant*, his first play, acted ; published 1669.
Marries Lady Elizabeth Howard, d. of Earl of Berkshire, December 1.

1665. *The Indian Emperor*, published 1667.
The Plague ; theatres closed from May 1665 to Christmas 1666.

1666. The Fire of London (September) ; Dryden at Charlton, Wiltshire.

1667. *Annus Mirabilis* (preface dated November 10, 1666).

1668. *Of Dramatic Poesy, an Essay* : see p. 199.
Dryden appointed Poet Laureate (April), in succession to Sir William Davenant.

1669. *Tyrannic Love* ; published 1670.

1670. *The Conquest of Granada* (two parts) ; published 1672.

1673. *Marriage à la Mode*.

1676. *Aureng-zebe*.

1678. *All for Love*.

1680. *Ovid's Epistles, Translated by Several Hands* (contains Preface and two epistles by Dryden).

1681. *The Spanish Friar*.
(November 17) *Absalom and Achitophel*.

1682. (March) *The Medal*.
(November 10) *Absalom and Achitophel, Second Part*.
(November 30) *Religio Laici*.
MacFlecknoe printed without authority : see p. 188.

1683. ' Life of Plutarch ' prefixed to *Plutarch's Lives, Translated by Several Hands*.

1684. *Miscellany Poems, by the most Eminent Hands* (contains the first authorized issue of *MacFlecknoe*, and translations from Ovid, Theocritus, and Virgil).
To the Memory of Mr. Oldham.

1685. (January) *Sylvae: or the Second Part of Poetical Miscellanies*
    (contains Preface and translations from Virgil, Lucretius,
    Theocritus, and Horace).

    Death of Charles II, February 5.

    (March) *Threnodia Augustalis.*

    Albion and Albanius, an Opera.

1686. Dryden joins the Roman Catholic Church.

    To the Memory of Mrs. Anne Killigrew.

1687. (April) *The Hind and the Panther.*

    (November) *A Song for St. Cecilia's Day.*

1688. (June) *Britannia Rediviva, a Poem on the Birth of the Prince.*
    William III lands at Torbay November 5, and reaches London
    December 19; James II escapes to France, December 23.

1689. William and Mary accept the throne, February 13.

    Dryden loses the laureateship; succeeded by Shadwell.

1690 *Don Sebastian, a Tragedy; Amphitryon, a Comedy.*

1691. *King Arthur, a Dramatic Opera.*

1692. (May) *Cleomenes, the Spartan Hero, a Tragedy.*

1693 (early, or late in 1692). *The Satires of Juvenal and Persius, made
    English* (begun 1690; prefatory 'Discourse', dated
    August 18, 1692).

    (February) 'A Character of Polybius and his Writings',
    prefixed to the translation of Polybius by Sir Henry Sheers.

    (July) *Examen Poeticum: Being the Third Part of Miscellany
    Poems* (contains Preface and translations from Ovid and
    Homer, and Songs).

1694. *To my dear Friend Mr. Congreve.*

    The Annual Miscellany (the fourth part of Miscellany Poems;
    contains translation of Virgil's Third Georgic, and the
    Epistle to Sir Godfrey Kneller).

    (March) *Love Triumphant,* his last play.

1695. (June) 'A Parallel betwixt Painting and Poetry', preface to
    a translation of Du Fresnoy's *De Arte Graphica.*

1697. (July) *The Works of Virgil, translated into English Verse*
    (undertaken 1693).

    (November) *Alexander's Feast.*

1700. (March) *Fables, Ancient and Modern* (begun 1698).

    The Secular Masque in Vanburgh's version of Fletcher's
    Pilgrim (published June 18).

    Dryden dies, May 1.

    Buried in Westminster Abbey, May 13.

CONGREVE'S

Character of Dryden

From the Dedication to Dryden's *Dramatic Works*, 1717

MR. DRYDEN had personal qualities to challenge both love and esteem from all who were truly acquainted with him.

He was of a nature exceedingly humane and compassionate ; easily forgiving injuries, and capable of a prompt and sincere reconciliation with them who had offended him.

Such a temperament is the only solid foundation of all moral virtues and sociable endowments. His friendship, where he professed it, went much beyond his professions ; and I have been told of strong and generous instances of it by the persons themselves who received them, though his hereditary income was little more than a bare competency.

As his reading had been very extensive, so was he very happy in a memory tenacious of everything that he had read. He was not more possessed of knowledge than he was communicative of it. But then his communication of it was by no means pedantic, or imposed upon the conversation ; but just such, and went so far as, by the natural turns of the discourse in which he was engaged, it was necessarily promoted or required. He was extreme ready and gentle in his correction of the errors of any writer who thought fit to consult him ; and full as ready and patient to admit of the reprehension of others in respect of his own oversight or mistakes. He was of very easy, I may say of very pleasing access ; but something slow and as it were diffident in his advances to others. He had something in his nature that abhorred intrusion into any society whatsoever. Indeed it is to be regretted that he was rather blameable in the other extreme; for by that means he was personally less known, and consequently his character might become liable both to misapprehensions and misrepresentations.

To the best of my knowledge and observation, he was, of all the men that ever I knew, one of the most modest, and the most easily to be discountenanced in his approaches
10 either to his superiors or his equals. . . .

As to his writings, I shall not take upon me to speak of them ; for to say little of them, would not be to do them right ; and to say all that I ought to say, would be to be very voluminous. But I may venture to say, in general terms, that no man hath written in our language so much, and so various matter, and in so various manners, so well. Another thing I may say very peculiar to him, which is, that his parts did not decline with his years, but that he was an improving writer to his last, even to near seventy
20 years of age, improving even in fire and imagination, as well as in judgment : witness his Ode on St. Cecilia's Day, and his Fables, his latest performances.

He was equally excellent in verse and in prose. His prose had all the clearness imaginable, together with all the nobleness of expression ; all the graces and ornaments proper and peculiar to it, without deviating into the language or diction of poetry. I make this observation, only to distinguish his style from that of many poetical writers, who, meaning to write harmoniously in prose, do
30 in truth often write mere blank verse.

I have heard him frequently own with pleasure, that if he had any talent for English prose, it was owing to his having often read the writings of the great Archbishop Tillotson.

His versification and his numbers he could learn of

nobody : for he first possessed those talents in perfection in our tongue. And they who have best succeeded in them since his time, have been indebted to his example ; and the more they have been able to imitate him, the better have they succeeded.

As his style in prose is always specifically different from his style in poetry, so, on the other hand, in his poems, his diction is, wherever his subject requires it, so sublimely and so truly poetical, that its essence, like that of pure gold, cannot be destroyed. Take his verses and divest them of 10 their rhymes, disjoint them in their numbers, transpose their expressions, make what arrangement and disposition you please of his words, yet shall there eternally be poetry, and something which will be found incapable of being resolved into absolute prose : an incontestable characteristic of a truly poetical genius.

I will say but one word more in general of his writings, which is, that what he has done in any one species, or distinct kind, would have been sufficient to have acquired him a great name. If he had written nothing but his 20 Prefaces, or nothing but his Songs, or his Prologues, each of them would have entitled him to the preference and distinction of excelling in his kind.

From JOHNSON'S

Life of Dryden

Published 1779

DRYDEN may be properly considered as the father of
English criticism, as the writer who first taught us to
determine upon principles the merit of composition. Of
our former poets the greatest dramatist wrote without
rules, conducted through life and nature by a genius that
rarely misled, and rarely deserted him. Of the rest, those
who knew the laws of propriety had neglected to teach
them. . . .

The dialogue on the Drama was one of his first essays
10 of criticism, written when he was yet a timorous candidate
for reputation, and therefore laboured with that diligence
which he might allow himself somewhat to remit, when his
name gave sanction to his positions, and his awe of the
public was abated, partly by custom, and partly by success.
It will not be easy to find, in all the opulence of our language, a treatise so artfully variegated with successive
representations of opposite probabilities, so enlivened with
imagery, so brightened with illustrations. His portraits
of the English dramatists are wrought with great spirit and
20 diligence. The account of Shakespeare may stand as a
perpetual model of encomiastic criticism ; exact without
minuteness, and lofty without exaggeration. The praise
lavished by Longinus, on the attestation of the heroes of
Marathon by Demosthenes, fades away before it. In
a few lines is exhibited a character so extensive in its comprehension, and so curious in its limitations, that nothing
can be added, diminished, or reformed ; nor can the
editors and admirers of Shakespeare, in all their emulation

of reverence, boast of much more than of having diffused and paraphrased this epitome of excellence, of having changed Dryden's gold for baser metal, of lower value though of greater bulk. . . .

As he had studied with great diligence the art of poetry, and enlarged or rectified his notions by experience perpetually increasing, he had his mind stored with principles and observations ; he poured out his knowledge with little labour ; for of labour, notwithstanding the multiplicity of his productions, there is sufficient reason to suspect that 10 he was not a lover. To write *con amore*, with fondness for the employment, with perpetual touches and retouches, with unwillingness to take leave of his own idea, and an unwearied pursuit of unattainable perfection, was, I think, no part of his character. . . .

His works abound with knowledge, and sparkle with illustrations. There is scarcely any science or faculty that does not supply him with occasional images and lucky similitudes ; every page discovers a mind very widely acquainted both with art and nature, and in full possession 20 of great stores of intellectual wealth. Of him that knows much it is natural to suppose that he has read with diligence ; yet I rather believe that the knowledge of Dryden was gleaned from accidental intelligence and various conversation, by a quick apprehension, a judicious selection, and a happy memory, a keen appetite of knowledge, and a powerful digestion ; by vigilance that permitted nothing to pass without notice, and a habit of reflection that suffered nothing useful to be lost. A mind like Dryden's, always curious, always active, to which every under- 30 standing was proud to be associated, and of which every one solicited the regard, by an ambitious display of himself, had a more pleasant, perhaps a nearer way, to knowledge than by the silent progress of solitary reading. I do not suppose that he despised books, or intentionally neglected

them ; but that he was carried out, by the impetuosity of
his genius, to more vivid and speedy instructors ; and
that his studies were rather desultory and fortuitous than
constant and systematical.

It must be confessed that he scarcely ever appears to
want book-learning but when he mentions books ; and to
him may be transferred the praise which he gives his
master Charles .

> His conversation, wit, and parts,
> His knowledge in the noblest useful arts,
> > Were such, dead authors could not give,
> > But habitudes of those that live ;
> Who, lighting him, did greater lights receive :
> He drain'd from all, and all they knew,
> His apprehension quick, his judgement true :
> That the most learn'd with shame confess
> His knowledge more, his reading only less.

Of all this, however, if the proof be demanded, I will not
undertake to give it ; the atoms of probability, of which
my opinion has been formed, lie scattered over all his
works ; and by him who thinks the question worth his
notice, his works must be perused with very close attention.

Criticism, either didactic or defensive, occupies almost
all his prose, except those pages which he has devoted to
his patrons ; but none of his prefaces were ever thought
tedious.   They have not the formality of a settled style,
in which the first half of the sentence betrays the other.
The clauses are never balanced, nor the periods modelled ;
every word seems to drop by chance, though it falls into
its proper place.   Nothing is cold or languid ; the whole is
airy, animated, and vigorous ; what is little, is gay ; what
is great, is splendid.   He may be thought to mention himself
too frequently ;   but while he forces himself upon our
esteem, we cannot refuse him to stand high in his own.
Every thing is excused by the play of images and the
spriteliness of expression.   Though all is easy, nothing is

feeble ; though all seems careless, there is nothing harsh ; and though, since his earlier works, more than a century has passed, they have nothing yet uncouth or obsolete.

He who writes much will not easily escape a manner, such a recurrence of particular modes as may be easily noted. Dryden is always *another and the same*, he does not exhibit a second time the same elegances in the same form, nor appears to have any art other than that of expressing with clearness what he thinks with vigour. His style could not easily be imitated, either seriously or ludicrously ; for, being always equable and always varied, it has no prominent or discriminative characters. The beauty who is totally free from disproportion of parts and features, cannot be ridiculed by an overcharged resemblance.

From his prose, however, Dryden derives only his accidental and secondary praise ; the veneration with which his name is pronounced by every cultivator of English literature is paid to him as he refined the language, improved the sentiments, and tuned the numbers of English poetry.

After about half a century of forced thoughts, and rugged metre, some advances towards nature and harmony had been already made by Waller and Denham ; they had shown that long discourses in rhyme grew more pleasing when they were broken into couplets, and that verse consisted not only in the number but the arrangement of syllables.

But though they did much, who can deny that they left much to do ? Their works were not many, nor were their minds of very ample comprehension. More examples of more modes of composition were necessary for the establishment of regularity, and the introduction of propriety in word and thought.

Every language of a learned nation necessarily divides itself into diction scholastic and popular, grave and familiar, elegant and gross ; and from a nice distinction of these different parts arises a great part of the beauty of style. But if we except a few minds, the favourites of nature, to whom their own original rectitude was in the place of rules, this delicacy of selection was little known to our authors ; our speech lay before them in a heap of confusion, and every man took for every purpose what chance might offer him.

There was therefore before the time of Dryden no poetical
10 diction, no system of words at once refined from the grossness of domestic use, and free from the harshness of terms appropriated to particular arts. Words too familiar, or too remote, defeat the purpose of a poet. From those sounds which we hear on small or on coarse occasions, we do not easily receive strong impressions, or delightful images ; and words to which we are nearly strangers, whenever they occur, draw that attention on themselves which they should transmit to things.

Those happy combinations of words which distinguish
20 poetry from prose, had been rarely attempted ; we had few elegances or flowers of speech, the roses had not yet been plucked from the bramble, or different colours had not been joined to enliven one another.

It may be doubted whether Waller and Denham could have overborne the prejudices which had long prevailed, and which even then were sheltered by the protection of Cowley. The new versification, as it was called, may be considered as owing its establishment to Dryden ; from whose time it is apparent that English poetry has had no
30 tendency to relapse to its former savageness.

The affluence and comprehension of our language is very illustriously displayed in our poetical translations of ancient writers ; a work which the French seem to relinquish in despair, and which we were long unable to perform with dexterity. Ben Jonson thought it necessary to copy

Horace almost word by word ; Feltham, his contemporary and adversary, considers it as indispensably requisite in a translation to give line for line. It is said that Sandys, whom Dryden calls the best versifier of the last age, has struggled hard to comprise every book of his English *Metamorphoses* in the same number of verses with the original. Holyday had nothing in view but to show that he understood his author, with so little regard to the grandeur of his diction, or the volubility of his numbers, that his metres can hardly be called verses ; they cannot 10 be read without reluctance, nor will the labour always be rewarded by understanding them. Cowley saw that such *copiers* were a *servile race* ; he asserted his liberty, and spread his wings so boldly that he left his authors. It was reserved for Dryden to fix the limits of poetical liberty, and give us just rules and examples of translation.

When languages are formed upon different principles, it is impossible that the same modes of expression should always be elegant in both. While they run on together, the closest translation may be considered as the best ; but 20 when they divaricate, each must take its natural course. Where correspondence cannot be obtained, it is necessary to be content with something equivalent. *Translation therefore*, says Dryden, *is not so loose as paraphrase, nor so close as metaphrase.*

All polished languages have different styles ; the concise, the diffuse, the lofty, and the humble. In the proper choice of style consists the resemblance which Dryden principally exacts from the translator. He is to exhibit his author's thoughts in such a dress of diction as the author would have 30 given them, had his language been English : rugged magnificence is not to be softened : hyperbolical ostentation is not to be repressed, nor sententious affectation to have its points blunted. A translator is to be like his author : it is not his business to excel him. . . .

It seldom happens that all the necessary causes concur to any great effect: will is wanting to power, or power to will, or both are impeded by external obstructions. The exigences in which Dryden was condemned to pass his life are reasonably supposed to have blasted his genius, to have driven out his works in a state of immaturity, and to have intercepted the full-blown elegance which longer growth would have supplied.

Poverty, like other rigid powers, is sometimes too hastily
10 accused. If the excellence of Dryden's works was lessened by his indigence, their number was increased ; and I know not how it will be proved, that if he had written less he would have written better ; or that indeed he would have undergone the toil of an author, if he had not been solicited by something more pressing than the love of praise.

But as is said by his Sebastian,

What had been, is unknown ; what is, appears.

We know that Dryden's several productions were so many successive expedients for his support ; his plays were
20 therefore often borrowed, and his poems were almost all occasional.

In an occasional performance no height of excellence can be expected from any mind, however fertile in itself, and however stored with acquisitions. He whose work is general and arbitrary has the choice of his matter, and takes that which his inclination and his studies have best qualified him to display and decorate. He is at liberty to delay his publication till he has satisfied his friends and himself ; till he has reformed his first thoughts by subse-
30 quent examination, and polished away those faults which the precipitance of ardent composition is likely to leave behind it. Virgil is related to have poured out a great number of lines in the morning, and to have passed the day in reducing them to fewer.

The occasional poet is circumscribed by the narrowness of his subject. Whatever can happen to man has happened so often that little remains for fancy or invention. We have been all born ; we have most of us been married ; and so many have died before us that our deaths can supply but few materials for a poet. In the fate of princes the public has an interest ; and what happens to them of good or evil, the poets have always considered as business for the Muse. But after so many inauguratory gratulations, nuptial hymns, and funeral dirges, he must be highly favoured by 10 nature, or by fortune, who says any thing not said before. Even war and conquest, however splendid, suggest no new images ; the triumphal chariot of a victorious monarch can be decked only with those ornaments that have graced his predecessors.

Not only matter but time is wanting. The poem must not be delayed till the occasion is forgotten. The lucky moments of animated imagination cannot be attended ; elegances and illustrations cannot be multiplied by gradual accumulation : the composition must be dispatched while 20 conversation is yet busy, and admiration fresh ; and haste is to be made, lest some other event should lay hold upon mankind.

Occasional compositions may however secure to a writer the praise both of learning and facility ; for they cannot be the effect of long study, and must be furnished immediately from the treasures of the mind. . . .

Absalom and Achitophel is a work so well known that particular criticism is superfluous. If it be considered as a poem political and controversial, it will be found to com- 30 prise all the excellences of which the subject is susceptible ; acrimony of censure, elegance of praise, artful delineation of characters, variety and vigour of sentiment, happy turns of language, and pleasing harmony of numbers ; and all these raised to such a height as can scarcely be found in any other English composition.

It is not, however, without faults ; some lines are inelegant or improper, and too many are irreligiously licentious. The original structure of the poem was defective ; allegories drawn to great length will always break ; Charles could not run continually parallel with David.

The subject had likewise another inconvenience : it admitted little imagery or description, and a long poem of
10 mere sentiments easily becomes tedious ; though all the parts are forcible, and every line kindles new rapture, the reader, if not relieved by the interposition of something that soothes the fancy, grows weary of admiration, and defers the rest.

As an approach to historical truth was necessary, the action and catastrophe were not in the poet's power ; there is therefore an unpleasing disproportion between the beginning and the end. We are alarmed by a faction formed out of many sects various in their principles, but agreeing in
20 their purpose of mischief, formidable for their numbers, and strong by their supports, while the king's friends are few and weak. The chiefs on either part are set forth to view ; but when expectation is at the height, the king makes a speech, and

Henceforth a series of new times began.

Who can forbear to think of an enchanted castle, with a wide moat and lofty battlements, walls of marble and gates of brass, which vanishes at once into air when the destined knight blows his horn before it ?

30 In the second part, written by Tate, there is a long insertion, which, for poignancy of satire, exceeds any part of the former. Personal resentment, though no laudable motive to satire, can add great force to general principles. Self-love is a busy prompter.

The Medal, written upon the same principles with *Absalom and Achitophel*, but upon a narrower plan, gives less pleasure, though it discovers equal abilities in the writer. The superstructure cannot extend beyond the foundation ; a single character or incident cannot furnish as many ideas as a series of events or multiplicity of agents. This poem therefore, since time has left it to itself, is not much read, nor perhaps generally understood, yet it abounds with touches both of humorous and serious satire. The picture of a man whose propensions to mischief are 10 such that his best actions are but inability of wickedness, is very skilfully delineated and strongly coloured. . . .

The *Religio Laici*, which borrows its title from the *Religio Medici* of Browne, is almost the only work of Dryden which can be considered as a voluntary effusion ; in this, therefore, it might be hoped that the full effulgence of his genius would be found. But unhappily the subject is rather argumentative than poetical : he intended only a specimen of metrical disputation.

> And this unpolish'd rugged verse I chose,   20
> As fittest for discourse, and nearest prose.

This, however, is a composition of great excellence in its kind, in which the familiar is very properly diversified with the solemn, and the grave with the humorous ; in which metre has neither weakened the force, nor clouded the perspicuity of argument ; nor will it be easy to find another example equally happy of this middle kind of writing, which though prosaic in some parts, rises to high poetry in others, and neither towers to the skies, nor creeps along the ground.

Of the same kind, or not far distant from it, is the *Hind* 30 *and Panther*, the longest of all Dryden's original poems ; an allegory intended to comprise and to decide the controversy between the Romanists and Protestants. The scheme of the work is injudicious and incommodious ; for what can

be more absurd than that one beast should counsel another
to rest her faith upon a pope and council ? He seems well
enough skilled in the usual topics of argument, endeavours
to show the necessity of an infallible judge, and reproaches
the Reformers with want of unity ; but is weak enough to
ask, why, since we see without knowing how, we may not
have an infallible judge without knowing where. . . .

Pope, whose judgement was perhaps a little bribed by the
subject, used to mention this poem as the most correct
10 specimen of Dryden's versification. It was indeed written
when he had completely formed his manner, and may be
supposed to exhibit, negligence excepted, his deliberate
and ultimate scheme of metre.

We may therefore reasonably infer that he did not
approve the perpetual uniformity which confines the sense
to couplets, since he has broken his lines in the initial
paragraph :

> A milk-white Hind, immortal and unchang'd,
> Fed on the lawns, and in the forest rang'd ;
20 > Without unspotted, innocent within,
> She fear'd no danger, for she knew no sin.
> Yet she had oft been chas'd with horns and hounds
> And Scythian shafts, and many winged wounds
> Aim'd at her heart ; was often forc'd to fly,
> And doom'd to death, though fated not to die.

These lines are lofty, elegant, and musical, notwithstanding the interruption of the pause, of which the effect
is rather increase of pleasure by variety than offence by
ruggedness. . . .

30 As it was by its nature a work of defiance, a composition which would naturally be examined with the utmost
acrimony of criticism, it was probably laboured with uncommon attention ; and there are, indeed, few negligences in
the subordinate parts. The original impropriety and the
subsequent unpopularity of the subject, added to the

ridiculousness of its first elements, has sunk it into neglect ; but it may be usefully studied as an example of poetical ratiocination, in which the argument suffers little from the metre. . . .

Of Juvenal there had been a translation by Stapylton, and another by Holyday ; neither of them is very poetical. Stapylton is more smooth, and Holyday's is more esteemed for the learning of his notes. A new version was proposed to the poets of that time, and undertaken by them in conjunction. The main design was conducted by Dryden, whose reputation was such that no man was unwilling to serve the Muses under him.

The general character of this translation will be given, when it is said to preserve the wit, but to want the dignity of the original. The peculiarity of Juvenal is a mixture of gaiety and stateliness, of pointed sentences and declamatory grandeur. His points have not been neglected, but his grandeur none of the band seemed to consider as necessary to be imitated, except Creech, who undertook the thirteenth satire. It is therefore perhaps possible to give a better representation of that great satirist, even in those parts which Dryden himself has translated, some passages excepted, which will never be excelled. . . .

Not long afterwards he undertook perhaps the most arduous work of its kind, a translation of Virgil, for which he had shown how well he was qualified by his version of the *Pollio*, and two episodes, one of Nisus and Euryalus, the other of Mezentius and Lausus.

In the comparison of Homer and Virgil, the discriminative excellence of Homer is elevation and comprehension of thought, and that of Virgil is grace and splendour of diction. The beauties of Homer are therefore difficult to be lost, and those of Virgil difficult to be retained. The massy trunk of sentiment is safe by its solidity, but the blossoms of elocution easily drop away. The author, having the choice of his

own images, selects those which he can best adorn : the
translator must, at all hazards, follow his original, and
express thoughts which perhaps he would not have chosen.
When to this primary difficulty is added the inconvenience
of a language so much inferior in harmony to the Latin, it
cannot be expected that they who read the *Georgics* and
the *Aeneid* should be much delighted with any version.

All these obstacles Dryden saw, and all these he determined to encounter.   The expectation of his work was
10 undoubtedly great ; the nation considered its honour as
interested in the event.   One gave him the different editions
of his author, and another helped him in the subordinate
parts.   The arguments of the several books were given him
by Addison.

The hopes of the public were not disappointed. He produced, says Pope, *the most noble and spirited translation
that I know in any language*.   It certainly excelled whatever had appeared in English, and appears to have satisfied
his friends, and, for the most part, to have silenced his
20 enemies. . . .

Since the English ear has been accustomed to the melli-
fluence of Pope's numbers, and the diction of poetry has
become more splendid, new attempts have been made to
translate Virgil ; and all his works have been attempted by
men better qualified to contend with Dryden.   I will not
engage myself in an invidious comparison by opposing one
passage to another ; a work of which there would be no
end, and which might be often offensive without use.

It is not by comparing line with line that the merit of
30 great works is to be estimated, but by their general effects
and ultimate result.   It is easy to note a weak line, and
write one more vigorous in its place ; to find a happiness of
expression in the original, and transplant it by force into
the version: but what is given to the parts may be sub-
ducted from the whole, and the reader may be weary,

though the critic may commend. Works of imagination excel by their allurement and delight ; by their power of attracting and detaining the attention. That book is good in vain which the reader throws away. He only is the master who keeps the mind in pleasing captivity; whose pages are perused with eagerness, and in hope of new pleasure are perused again ; and whose conclusion is perceived with an eye of sorrow, such as the traveller casts upon departing day.

By his proportion of this predomination I will consent 10 that Dryden should be tried ; of this, which, in opposition to reason, makes Ariosto the darling and the pride of Italy ; of this,which, in defiance of criticism, continues Shakespeare the sovereign of the drama.

His last work was his *Fables*, in which he gave us the first example of a mode of writing which the Italians call *rifacimento*, a renovation of ancient writers, by modernizing their language. Thus the old poem of Boiardo has been new-dressed by Domenichi and Berni. The works of Chaucer, upon which this kind of rejuvenescence has been 20 bestowed by Dryden, require little criticism. The tale of the Cock seems hardly worth revival ; and the story of Palamon and Arcite, containing an action unsuitable to the times in which it is placed, can hardly be suffered to pass without censure of the hyperbolical commendation which Dryden has given it in the general Preface, and in a poetical Dedication, a piece where his original fondness of remote conceits seems to have revived.

Of the three pieces borrowed from Boccace, *Sigismunda* may be defended by the celebrity of the story. *Theodore* 30 *and Honoria*, though it contains not much moral, yet afforded opportunities of striking description. And *Cymon* was formerly a tale of such reputation, that, at the revival of letters, it was translated into Latin by one of the Beroalds.

Whatever subjects employed his pen, he was still improving our measures and embellishing our language.

In this volume are interspersed some short original poems, which, with his prologues, epilogues, and songs, may be comprised in Congreve's remark, that even those, if he had written nothing else, would have entitled him to the praise of excellence in his kind.

One composition must however be distinguished. The *Ode for St. Cecilia's Day,* perhaps the last effort of his
10 poetry, has been always considered as exhibiting the highest flight of fancy and the exactest nicety of art. This is allowed to stand without a rival. If indeed there is any excellence beyond it, in some other of Dryden's works that excellence must be found. Compared with the *Ode on Killigrew* it may be pronounced perhaps superior in the whole ; but without any single part equal to the first stanza of the other.

It is said to have cost Dryden a fortnight's labour ; but it does not want its negligences : some of the lines are
20 without correspondent rhymes ; a defect which I never detected but after an acquaintance of many years, and which the enthusiasm of the writer might hinder him from perceiving.

His last stanza has less emotion than the former ; but is not less elegant in the diction. The conclusion is vicious ; the music of Timotheus, which *raised a mortal to the skies,* had only a metaphorical power ; that of Cecilia, which *drew an angel down,* had a real effect : the crown therefore could not reasonably be divided.

30 IN a general survey of Dryden's labours, he appears to have a mind very comprehensive by nature, and much enriched with acquired knowledge. His compositions are the effects of a vigorous genius operating upon large materials.

The power that predominated in his intellectual operations was rather strong reason than quick sensibility.
Upon all occasions that were presented he studied rather
than felt, and produced sentiments not such as nature
enforces, but meditation supplies. With the simple and
elemental passions, as they spring separate in the mind,
he seems not much acquainted ; and seldom describes
them but as they are complicated by the various relations
of society and confused in the tumults and agitations of
life.   10

What he says of love may contribute to the explanation
of his character :

> Love various minds does variously inspire ;
> It stirs in gentle bosoms gentle fire,
> Like that of incense on the altar laid ;
> But raging flames tempestuous souls invade ;
> A fire which every windy passion blows,
> With pride it mounts, or with revenge it glows.

Dryden's was not one of the *gentle bosoms* : Love, as it
subsists in itself, with no tendency but to the person loved, 20
and wishing only for correspondent kindness ; such love as
shuts out all other interest ; the Love of the Golden Age, was
too soft and subtle to put his faculties in motion. He hardly
conceived it but in its turbulent effervescence with some
other desires ; when it was inflamed by rivalry, or
obstructed by difficulties ; when it invigorated ambition,
or exasperated revenge.

He is therefore, with all his variety of excellence, not
often pathetic ; and had so little sensibility of the power
of effusions purely natural, that he did not esteem them 30
in others. Simplicity gave him no pleasure ; and for the
first part of his life he looked on Otway with contempt,
though at last, indeed very late, he confessed that in his
play *there* was *nature, which is the chief beauty*.

We do not always know our own motives. I am not

certain whether it was not rather the difficulty which he found in exhibiting the genuine operations of the heart, than a servile submission to an injudicious audience, that filled his plays with false magnificence. It was necessary to fix attention ; and the mind can be captivated only by recollection, or by curiosity ; by reviving natural sentiments, or impressing new appearances of things : sentences were readier at his call than images ; he could more easily fill the ear with some splendid novelty, than awaken
10 those ideas that slumber in the heart.

The favourite exercise of his mind was ratiocination ; and, that argument might not be too soon at an end, he delighted to talk of liberty and necessity, destiny and contingence ; these he discusses in the language of the school with so much profundity that the terms which he uses are not always understood. It is indeed learning, but learning out of place.

When once he had engaged himself in disputation, thoughts flowed in on either side : he was now no longer
20 at a loss ; he had always objections and solutions at command : *verbaque provisam rem*—give him matter for his verse, and he finds without difficulty verse for his matter.

In Comedy, for which he professes himself not naturally qualified, the mirth which he excites will perhaps not be found so much to arise from any original humour, or peculiarity of character nicely distinguished and diligently pursued, as from incidents and circumstances, artifices and surprises ; from jests of action rather than of sentiment. What he had of humorous or passionate, he seems to have
30 had not from nature, but from other poets ; if not always as a plagiary, at least as an imitator.

Next to argument, his delight was in wild and daring sallies of sentiment, in the irregular and eccentric violence of wit. He delighted to tread upon the brink of meaning, where light and darkness begin to mingle ; to approach the precipice of absurdity, and hover over the abyss of unideal vacancy. . . .

These bursts of extravagance Dryden calls the *Dalilahs* of the Theatre, and owns that many noisy lines of Maximin and Almanzor call out for vengeance upon him ; but I *knew*, says he, *that they were bad enough to please, even when I wrote them.* There is surely reason to suspect that he pleased himself as well as his audience ; and that these, like the harlots of other men, had his love, though not his approbation. . . . 10

These are his faults of affectation ; his faults of negligence are beyond recital. Such is the unevenness of his compositions, that ten lines are seldom found together without something of which the reader is ashamed. Dryden was no rigid judge of his own pages ; he seldom struggled after supreme excellence, but snatched in haste what was within his reach ; and when he could content others, was himself contented. He did not keep present to his mind an idea of pure perfection, nor compare his works, such as they were, with what they might be made. He knew to whom he 20 should be opposed. He had more music than Waller, more vigour than Denham, and more nature than Cowley ; and from his contemporaries he was in no danger. Standing therefore in the highest place, he had no care to rise by contending with himself ; but while there was no name above his own, was willing to enjoy fame on the easiest terms.

He was no lover of labour. What he thought sufficient he did not stop to make better, and allowed himself to leave many parts unfinished, in confidence that the good lines 30 would overbalance the bad. What he had once written he dismissed from his thoughts ; and, I believe, there is no example to be found of any correction or improvement made by him after publication. The hastiness of his productions might be the effect of necessity ; but his subsequent neglect could hardly have any other cause than impatience of study.

What can be said of his versification will be little more than a dilatation of the praise given it by Pope :

> Waller was smooth ; by Dryden taught to join
> The varying verse, the full-resounding line,
> The long majestic march, and energy divine.

Some improvements had been already made in English numbers, but the full force of our language was not yet felt ; the verse that was smooth was commonly feeble. If Cowley had sometimes a finished line, he had it by chance. Dryden knew how to choose the flowing and the sonorous words ; to vary the pauses, and adjust the accents ; to diversify the cadence, and yet preserve the smoothness of his metre. . . .

Of Dryden's works it was said by Pope, that *he could select from them better specimens of every mode of poetry than any other English writer could supply.* Perhaps no nation ever produced a writer that enriched his language with such variety of models. To him we owe the improvement, perhaps the completion of our metre, the refinement of our language, and much of the correctness of our sentiments. By him we were taught *sapere et fari,* to think naturally and express forcibly. Though Davies has reasoned in rhyme before him, it may be perhaps maintained that he was the first who joined argument with poetry. He showed us the true bounds of a translator's liberty. What was said of Rome, adorned by Augustus, may be applied by an easy metaphor to English poetry embellished by Dryden, *lateritiam invenit, marmoream reliquit,* he found it brick, and he left it marble.

Life of Dryden

Published 1808

THE early habits of Dryden's education and poetical studies gave his researches somewhat too much of a metaphysical character ; and it was a consequence of his mental acuteness, that his dramatic personages often philosophized or reasoned, when they ought only to have felt. The more lofty, the fiercer, the more ambitious feelings, seem also to have been his favourite studies. Perhaps the analytical mode in which he exercised his studies of human life tended to confine his observation to the more energetic feelings of pride, anger, ambition, and other high-toned passions. He that mixes in public life must see enough of these stormy convulsions ; but the finer and more imperceptible operations of love, in its sentimental modifications, if the heart of the author does not supply an example from its own feelings, cannot easily be studied at the expense of others. Dryden's bosom, it must be owned, seems to have afforded him no such means of information ; the licence of his age, and perhaps the advanced period at which he commenced his literary career, had probably armed him against this more exalted strain of passion. The love of the senses he has in many places expressed, in as forcible and dignified colouring as the subject could admit ; but of a mere moral and sentimental passion he seems to have had little idea, since he frequently substitutes in its place the absurd, unnatural, and fictitious refinements of romance. In short, his love is always in indecorous nakedness, or sheathed in the stiff panoply of chivalry. The most pathetic verses which Dryden has composed, are unquestionably contained

in the epistle to Congreve, where he recommends his
laurels, in such moving terms, to the care of his surviving
friend.   The quarrel and reconciliation of Sebastian and
Dorax is also full of the noblest emotion.   In both cases,
however, the interest is excited by means of masculine
and exalted passion, not of those which arise from the
mere delicate sensibilities of our nature ; and, to use
a Scottish phrase, ' bearded men ' weep at them, rather
than Horace's audience of youths and maidens.

10   But if Dryden fails in expressing the milder and more
tender passions, not only did the stronger feelings of the
heart, in all its dark or violent workings, but the face
of natural objects, and their operation upon the human
mind, pass promptly in review at his command.   External
pictures, and their corresponding influence on the spectator,
are equally ready at his summons ; and though his poetry,
from the nature of his subjects, is in general rather ethic
and didactic, than narrative, yet no sooner does he adopt
the latter style of composition, than his figures and his
20 landscapes are presented to the mind with the same
vivacity as the flow of his reasoning, or the acute metaphysical discrimination of his characters.

Still the powers of observation and of deduction are
not the only qualities essential to the poetical character.
The philosopher may indeed prosecute his experimental
researches into the *arcana* of nature, and announce them
to the public through the medium of a friendly *redacteur*,
as the legislator of Israel obtained permission to speak to
the people by the voice of Aaron ; but the poet has no
30 such privilege ; nay, his doom is so far capricious, that,
though he may be possessed of the primary quality of
poetical conception to the highest possible extent, it is
but like a lute without its strings, unless he has the
subordinate, though equally essential, power of expressing
what he feels and conceives, in appropriate and harmonious

language. With this power Dryden's poetry was gifted, in a degree surpassing in modulated harmony that of all who had preceded him, and inferior to none that has since written English verse. He first showed that the English language was capable of uniting smoothness and strength. The hobbling verses of his predecessors were abandoned even by the lowest versifiers ; and by the force of his precept and example, the meanest lampooners of the year seventeen hundred wrote smoother lines than Donne and Cowley, the chief poets of the earlier half of the seventeenth century. What was said of Rome adorned by Augustus, has been, by Johnson, applied to English poetry improved by Dryden ; that he found it of brick, and left it of marble. This reformation was not merely the effect of an excellent ear, and a superlative command of gratifying it by sounding language ; it was, we have seen, the effect of close, accurate, and continued study of the power of the English tongue. . . .

In lyrical poetry Dryden must be allowed to have no equal. *Alexander's Feast* is sufficient to show his supremacy in that brilliant department. In this exquisite production he flung from him all the trappings with which his contemporaries had embarrassed the ode. The language, lofty and striking as the ideas are, is equally simple and harmonious ; without far-fetched allusions, or epithets, or metaphors, the story is told as intelligibly as if it had been in the most humble prose. The change of tone in the harp of Timotheus regulates the measure and the melody and the language of every stanza. The hearer, while he is led on by the successive changes, experiences almost the feelings of the Macedonian and his peers ; nor is the splendid poem disgraced by one word or line unworthy of it, unless we join in the severe criticism of Dr. Johnson on the concluding stanzas. . . .

The satirical powers of Dryden were of the highest order. He draws his arrow to the head, and dismisses it

straight upon his object of aim. In this walk he wrought
almost as great a reformation as upon versification in
general ; as will plainly appear, if we consider that the
satire, before Dryden's time, bore the same reference to
Absalom and Achitophel which an ode of Cowley bears to
Alexander's Feast. Butler, and his imitators, had adopted
a metaphysical satire, as the poets in the earlier part of
the century had created a metaphysical vein of serious
poetry. Both required store of learning to supply the
10 perpetual expenditure of extraordinary and far-fetched
illustration ; the object of both was to combine and hunt
down the strangest and most fanciful analogies ; and
both held the attention of the reader perpetually on the
stretch, to keep up with the meaning of the author. There
can be no doubt that this metaphysical vein was much
better fitted for the burlesque than the sublime. Yet the
perpetual scintillation of Butler's wit is too dazzling to be
delightful ; and we can seldom read far in *Hudibras* without
feeling more fatigue than pleasure. His fancy is employed
20 with the profusion of a spendthrift, by whose eternal
round of banquetting his guests are at length rather
wearied out than regaled. Dryden was destined to correct
this among other errors of his age ; to show the difference
between burlesque and satire ; and to teach his successors
in that species of assault, rather to thrust than to flourish
with their weapon. For this purpose he avoided the
unvaried and unrelieved style of grotesque description and
combination, which had been fashionable since the satires
of Cleveland and Butler. To render the objects of his
30 satire hateful and contemptible, he thought it necessary
to preserve the lighter shades of character, if not for the
purpose of softening the portrait, at least for that of pre-
serving the likeness. While Dryden seized, and dwelt
upon, and aggravated, all the evil features of his subject,
he carefully retained just as much of its laudable traits as

preserved him from the charge of want of candour, and
fixed down the resemblance upon the party. And thus,
instead of unmeaning caricatures, he presents portraits
which cannot be mistaken, however unfavourable ideas
they may convey of the originals. The character of Shaftesbury, both as Achitophel and as drawn in *The Medal*,
bears peculiar witness to this assertion. While other court
poets endeavoured to turn the obnoxious statesman into
ridicule, on account of his personal infirmities and extravagancies, Dryden boldly confers upon him all the praise 10
for talent and for genius that his friends could have claimed,
and trusts to the force of his satirical expression for working
up even these admirable attributes with such a mixture of
evil propensities and dangerous qualities, that the whole
character shall appear dreadful, and even hateful, but not
contemptible. . . .

The *Fables* of Dryden are the best examples of his talents
as a narrative poet ; those powers of composition, description, and narration, which must have been called into
exercise by the Epic Muse, had his fate allowed him to 20
enlist among her votaries. . . .

Upon the whole, in introducing these romances of
Boccaccio and Chaucer to modern readers, Dryden has
necessarily deprived them of some of the charms which
they possess for those who have perused them in their
original state. With a tale or poem, by which we have been
sincerely interested, we connect many feelings independent
of those arising from actual poetical merit. The delight,
arising from the whole, sanctions, nay sanctifies, the faulty
passages ; and even actual improvements, like supple- 30
ments to a mutilated statue of antiquity, injure our pre-
conceived associations, and hurt, by their incongruity
with our feelings, more than they give pleasure by their
own excellence. But to antiquaries Dryden has sufficiently justified himself, by declaring his version made for

the sake of modern readers, who understand sense and poetry as well as the 'old Saxon' admirers of Chaucer, when that poetry and sense are put into words which they can understand.   Let us also grant him, that, for the beauties which are lost, he has substituted many which the original did not afford ; that, in passages of gorgeous description, he has added even to the chivalrous splendour of Chaucer, and has graced with poetical ornament the simplicity of Boccaccio ; that, if he has failed in tenderness,
10 he is never deficient in majesty; and that, if the heart be sometimes untouched, the understanding and fancy are always exercised and delighted. . . .

The prose of Dryden may rank with the best in the English language.   It is no less of his own formation than his versification, is equally spirited, and equally harmonious. Without the lengthened and pedantic sentences of Clarendon, it is dignified where dignity is becoming, and is lively without the accumulation of strained and absurd allusions and metaphors, which were unfortu-
20 nately mistaken for wit by many of the author's contemporaries. . . .

The gleams of philosophical spirit which so frequently illumine these pages of criticism ; the lively and appro- priate grace of illustration ; the true and correct expression of the general propositions ; the simple and unaffected passages, in which, when led to allude to his personal labours and situation, he mingles the feelings of the man with the instructions of the critic—unite to render Dryden's Essays the most delightful prose in the English
30 language.

From HAZLITT'S

Lecture on Dryden

Lectures on the English Poets, 1818

DRYDEN was a better prose-writer, and a bolder and
more varied versifier, than Pope. He was a more vigorous
thinker, a more correct and logical declaimer, and had
more of what may be called strength of mind than Pope ;
but he had not the same refinement and delicacy of feeling.
Dryden's eloquence and spirit were possessed in a higher
degree by others, and in nearly the same degree by Pope
himself ; but that by which Pope was distinguished was
an essence which he alone possessed, and of incomparable
value on that sole account. Dryden's Epistles are excellent, 10
but inferior to Pope's, though they appear (particularly the
admirable one to Congreve) to have been the model on
which the latter formed his. His Satires are better than
Pope's. His *Absalom and Achitophel* is superior, both in
force of invective and discrimination of character, to anything of Pope's in the same way. The character of Achitophel is very fine, and breathes, if not a sincere love for
virtue, a strong spirit of indignation against vice.

MacFlecknoe is the origin of the idea of *The Dunciad* ;
but it is less elaborately constructed, less feeble, and less 20
heavy. The difference between Pope's satirical portraits
and Dryden's appears to be this in a good measure, that
Dryden seems to grapple with his antagonists, and to
describe real persons ; Pope seems to refine upon them in
his own mind, and to make them out just what he pleases,
till they are not real characters, but the mere drivelling
effusions of his spleen and malice. Pope describes the thing,
and then goes on describing his own description till he loses

himself in verbal repetitions. Dryden recurs to the object
often, takes fresh sittings of nature, and gives us new
strokes of character as well as of his pencil. *The Hind
and Panther* is an allegory as well as a satire ; and so
far it tells less home ; the battery is not so point-blank.
But otherwise it has more genius, vehemence, and strength
of description than any other of Dryden's works, not
excepting the *Absalom and Achitophel*. It also contains
the finest examples of varied and sounding versification. . . .
10   The *Annus Mirabilis* is a tedious performance ; it is
a tissue of far-fetched, heavy, lumbering conceits, and in
the worst style of what has been denominated metaphysical poetry.   His Odes in general are of the same
stamp ; they are the hard-strained offspring of a meagre,
meretricious fancy. The famous *Ode on St. Cecilia* deserves
its reputation ; for, as a piece of poetical mechanism to
be set to music, or recited in alternate strophe and anti-
strophe, with classical allusions, and flowing verse, nothing
can be better. It is equally fit to be said or sung ; it is
20 not equally good to read. It is lyrical, without being
epic or dramatic. For instance, the description of Bacchus,

> The jolly god in triumph comes,
> Sound the trumpets, beat the drums ;
> Flush'd with a purple grace,
> He shows his honest face—

does not answer, as it ought, to our idea of the God, return-
ing from the conquest of India, with satyrs and wild beasts
that he had tamed following in his train ; crowned with
vine leaves, and riding in a chariot drawn by leopards—
30 such as we have seen him painted by Titian or Rubens !
Lyrical poetry, of all others, bears the nearest resemblance
to painting : it deals in hieroglyphics and passing figures,
which depend for effect, not on the working out, but on the
selection. It is the dance and pantomime of poetry.   In
variety and rapidity of movement, the *Alexander's Feast*

has all that can be required in this respect ; it wants only loftiness and truth of character. . . .

His alterations from Chaucer and Boccaccio show a greater knowledge of the taste of his readers and power of pleasing them, than acquaintance with the genius of his authors. He ekes out the lameness of the verse in the former, and breaks the force of the passion in both. The *Tancred and Sigismunda* is the only general exception, in which, I think, he has fully retained, if not improved upon, the impassioned declamation of the original. The *Honoria* has none of the bewildered, dreary, preternatural effect of Boccaccio's story. Nor has *The Flower and the Leaf* anything of the enchanting simplicity and concentrated feeling of Chaucer's romantic fiction. Dryden, however, sometimes seemed to indulge himself as well as his readers, as in keeping entire that noble line in Palamon's address to Venus :

Thou gladder of the mount of Cithæron !

His Tales have been, upon the whole, the most popular of his works ; and I should think that a translation of some of the other serious tales in Boccaccio and Chaucer, as that of Isabella, the Falcon, of Constance, the Prioress's Tale, and others, if executed with taste and spirit, could not fail to succeed in the present day.

From GEORGE SAINTSBURY'S

DRYDEN

English Men of Letters Series, 1881

So long as any one holds a definition of poetry which regards it wholly or chiefly from the point of view of its subject-matter, wide differences are unavoidable. But if we hold what I venture to think the only Catholic faith with regard to it, that it consists not in a selection of subjects, but in a method of treatment, then it seems to me that all difficulty vanishes. We get out of the hopeless and sterile controversies as to whether Shelley was a greater poet than Dryden, or Dryden a greater poet than
10 Shelley. For my part, I yield to no man living in rational admiration for either, but I decline altogether to assign marks to each in a competitive examination. There are, as it seems to me, many mansions in poetry, and the great poets live apart in them. What constitutes a great poet is supremacy in his own line of poetical expression. Such supremacy must of course be shown in work of sufficient bulk and variety, on the principle that one swallow does not make a summer. We cannot call Lovelace a great poet, or Barnabe Barnes ; perhaps we cannot give the name
20 to Collins or to Gray. We must be satisfied that the poet has his faculty of expression well at command, not merely that it sometimes visits him in a casual manner ; and we must know that he can apply it in a sufficient number of different ways. But when we see that he can under these conditions exhibit pretty constantly the poetical *differentia*, the power of making the common uncommon by the use of articulate language in metrical arrangement so as to excite indefinite suggestions of beauty, then he must be acknowledged a master.

When we want to see whether a man is a great poet or not, let us take him in his commonplaces, and see what he does with them. Here are four lines which are among the last that Dryden wrote ; they occur in the address to the Duchess of Ormond, who was, it must be remembered, by birth Lady Margaret Somerset :

> O daughter of the rose, whose cheeks unite
> The differing titles of the red and white,
> Who heaven's alternate beauty well display,
> The blush of morning and the milky way. 10

The ideas contained in these lines are as old, beyond all doubt, as the practice of love-making between persons of the Caucasian type of physiognomy, and the images in which those ideas are expressed are in themselves as well worn as the stones of the Pyramids. But I maintain that any poetical critic worth his salt could, without knowing who wrote them, but merely from the arrangement of the words, the rhythm and cadence of the line, and the manner in which the images are presented, write ' This is a poet, and probably a great poet ', across them, and that he would 20 be right in doing so. When such a critic, in reading the works of the author of these lines, finds that the same touch is, if not invariably, almost always present ; that in the handling of the most unpromising themes, the *mots rayonnants*, the *mots de lumière* are never lacking ; that the suggested images of beauty never fail for long together ; then he is justified in striking out the ' probably ' and writing ' This is a great poet '. If he tries to go further, and to range his great poets in order of merit, he will almost certainly fail. He cannot count up the beauties in 30 one, and then the beauties in the other, and strike the balance accordingly. He can only say, ' There is the faculty of producing those beauties ; it is exercised under such conditions, and with such results, that there is no doubt of its being a native and resident faculty, not a

mere casual inspiration of the moment ; and this being so,
I pronounce the man a poet, and a great one '. This can
be said of Dryden, as it can be said of Shelley, or Spenser,
or Keats, to name only the great English poets who are
most dissimilar to him in subject and in style. All beyond
this is treacherous speculation. The critic quits the
assistance of a plain and catholic theory of poetry, and
develops all sorts of private judgements, and not improbably
private crotchets. The ideas which this poet works on
10 are more congenial to his ideas than the ideas which that
poet works on ; the dialect of one is softer to his ear than
the dialect of another ; very frequently some characteristic
which has not the remotest connexion with his poetical
merits or demerits makes the scale turn. Of only one
poet can it be safely said that he is greater than the other
great poets, for the reason that in Dryden's own words he
is larger and more comprehensive than any of them. But
with the exception of Shakespeare, the greatest poets in
different styles are, in the eyes of a sound poetical criticism,
20 very much on an equality. Dryden's peculiar gift, in
which no poet of any language has surpassed him, is
the faculty of treating any subject which he does treat
poetically. His range is enormous, and wherever it is
deficient, it is possible to see that external circumstances
had to do with the apparent limitation. That the author
of the tremendous satire of the political pieces should be
the author of the exquisite lyrics scattered about the plays ;
that the special pleader of *Religio Laici* should be the tale-
teller of *Palamon and Arcite*, are things which, the more
30 carefully I study other poets and their comparatively
limited perfection, astonish me the more.

From SIR WALTER RALEIGH'S

Lecture on

JOHN DRYDEN AND POLITICAL SATIRE

Delivered 1913, published 1923

ALL four of these great satires fall within a single year. Dryden was a well-known dramatist and poet, but he issued them all anonymously. They produced a sensation greater than any printed pamphlet had ever produced in England. I do not remember any other case of a pamphlet designed to achieve a particular end, pointed to the occasion, topical and allusive in every line, which gained at once, and retained ever after, a place among our great national classics. The effect it produced may be well measured by the poems written in its praise, while yet the author re- 10 mained unknown. The verse of *Absalom*, says Nathaniel Lee, is 'divinely good', each syllable is a soul. It is

As if a Milton from the dead arose,
Filed off the rust, and the right party chose. . . .

What these praises mean is that Dryden was recognized at once, as he is recognized still, for the first of the moderns. He 'filed off the rust'; he discarded the antique poetic trappings, and proved that poetry could do work in the world. I confess that when I look through the collected poems of Dryden I am amazed by his completely modern 20 attitude to all the old traditions. Take a trivial but significant instance. In *The Secular Masque* he introduces a chorus of the heathen divinities, who describe the changes that time has wrought in the world. Diana celebrates the sport of hunting beloved by the court of James I, and then joins with Janus, Chronos, and Momus, in a festive chorus :

Then our age was in its prime :
Free from rage and free from crime.
A very merry, dancing, drinking,
Laughing, quaffing, and unthinking time. 30

The whole masque resembles nothing so much as a Drury Lane pantomime. And Dryden's innovations in language were, to his own age, no less startling. He was content to make use of the colloquial speech of the day, the speech in which men traffic, and quarrel, and discuss, but he used it with such intensity and conciseness that he raised it to a higher power. The satirists who came before him had either beaten the air, like the Elizabethans, or had been fanciful, grotesque, and metaphysical, like Butler and Cleveland. They dressed themselves in cobwebs ; Dryden wore a suit of armour. Men of the world had been accustomed to deal with poetry as a very good thing in its own place, when you have the time and the taste for it. You cannot deal thus with what you fear. Dryden compelled them to find the time.

If any one protests that the highest poetry, like the purest mathematics, can do no work, I do not desire to quarrel with him, so long as no attempt is made to deprive Dryden of the name of a great poet. Among the many definitions of poetry it is wise to choose the broadest. To exclude from the name of poetry work which is artistically ordered in strong and polished verse by an imagination of extraordinary scope and power, is a wretched impoverishment of thought and of speech. . . .

One of the great fascinations of Dryden's satire is its perfect ease of application to our own time. The divisions of opinion, the foibles, and the characters that he describes are alive among us to-day. Only the power and the will to satirize them have grown feebler. One reason of this, no doubt, is that our differences, for all their violence, are less fundamental and less tragic. A generation which had seen the king of England led to the block was in no danger of under-estimating the gravity of political differences. Almost all the political problems of to-day bear a likeness to the problems of the seventeenth century ; but the colours of that earlier picture are darker and stronger. We are perhaps humaner than they ; we are certainly more humanitarian. We do not behead those who are opposed to us, we do not even condemn them ; we explain them. Explanation is a subtler kind of satire, and it is touched, as Dryden insisted that all good satire should be touched, with concession, and even with sympathy. But we have to pay for our gains ; and we have lost the grand style. . . .

The warfare of party has raged on, with varying fortunes, 10 for more than two hundred years since Dryden wielded his two-edged sword, and the honours are still divided. But it would be a mistake to regard Dryden as first and foremost a party man. No mere party pamphleteer ever has won, or ever could win, the place that he holds in English letters. He is of the centre ; his party is the party of Aristophanes and of Rabelais. His best work is inspired by the sanity that inhabits at the heart of things. He lived in a turbulent age, and he was a fighter. But all extremists are his natural enemies. His weapons can be used, on 20 occasion, by either side. He hated wrong-headed theorists and fanatics, who commonly impose their alliance, a heavy burden, on the reforming party in the State. He also hated all contented and self-sufficient dullards, who for the most part have to be supported, a grievous weight, by the party that stands for the established order. He makes war on both, with laughter that flashes and cuts. There are many provinces of poetry, some where poetry is most at home, that are strange to him. His love lyrics are, with very few exceptions, a miracle of banality. His best 30 dramas just fall short of greatness. But in prose criticism, as in argumentative verse, and in metrical satire, he has not been surpassed. Not many authors have achieved the highest rank in three such diverse kinds.

If Dryden has failed to captivate some lovers of poetry

it is perhaps because he deals, almost exclusively, with public affairs. Even religion is treated, throughout his argumentative poems, in one aspect only, as a public interest. Were it not for one or two allusions to his advancing years, his works would give you no clue to his private life and retired meditations. If war, politics, and argument were banished from the face of the earth, nothing would be left for him to say, or at any rate he would say nothing. Congreve remarked that Dryden was the most modest man he ever knew ; and certainly he is one of the most reserved of poets. He does not take his readers into his confidence ; he has no endearing indiscretions. He is content to meet them in an open place, where there is business enough to bespeak their attention. A professional man of letters, especially if he is much at war with unscrupulous enemies, is naturally jealous of his privacy ; he will be silent on his more personal interests, or, if he must speak, will veil them under conventional forms. So it was, I think, with Dryden ; he is no bosom friend, to be the companion of those who keep the world and its noises at a distance. Those who do not care for Dryden may well care for poetry ; it is difficult to believe that they can care for politics, war, or argument.

Selections from

D R Y D E N ' S

Poetry and Prose

HEROIC STANZAS,

Consecrated to the Memory of His Highness

OLIVER,

Late Lord Protector of this Commonwealth, &c.

WRITTEN AFTER THE CELEBRATING OF HIS FUNERAL

1659

(Stanzas 6, 7, 8, 10, 13, 18, 37)

HIS grandeur he derived from Heaven alone,
　For he was great, ere Fortune made him so ;
And wars, like mists that rise against the sun,
　Made him but greater seem, not greater grow.

No borrowed bays his temples did adorn,　　　　5
　But to our crown he did fresh jewels bring ;
Nor was his virtue poisoned, soon as born,
　With the too early thoughts of being king.

Fortune, that easy mistress of the young,
　But to her ancient servants coy and hard,　　10
Him at that age her favourites ranked among
　When she her best-loved Pompey did discard.

And yet dominion was not his design ;
　We owe that blessing not to him, but Heaven,
Which to fair acts unsought rewards did join,　15
　Rewards that less to him than us were given.

Swift and resistless through the land he passed,
　Like that bold Greek who did the East subdue,
And made to battles such heroic haste
　As if on wings of victory he flew.　　　　　　20

Nor was he like those stars which only shine
   When to pale mariners they storms portend ;
He had his calmer influence, and his mien
   Did love and majesty together blend.

His ashes in a peaceful urn shall rest ;   25
   His name a great example stands to show
How strangely high endeavours may be blessed
   Where piety and valour jointly go.

A S T R Æ A   R E D U X

A Poem on the happy

Restoration and Return

of His Sacred Majesty

Charles the Second

Published June 1660

(Lines 21–8, 276–91, 312–23)

For his long absence Church and State did groan ;
Madness the pulpit, faction seized the throne:
Experienced age in deep despair was lost
To see the rebel thrive, the loyal crost :
Youth that with joys had unacquainted been   5
Envied gray hairs that once good days had seen :
We thought our sires, not with their own content,
Had, ere we came to age, our portion spent. . . .

Methinks I see those crowds on Dover's strand,
Who in their haste to welcome you to land   10
Choked up the beach with their still growing store,
And made a wilder torrent on the shore :

While, spurred with eager thoughts of past delight,
Those who had seen you court a second sight,
Preventing still your steps and making haste   15
To meet you often wheresoe'er you past.
How shall I speak of that triumphant day
When you renewed the expiring pomp of May !
(A month that owns an interest in your name :
You and the flowers are its peculiar claim.)   20
That star, that at your birth shone out so bright
It stained the duller sun's meridian light,
Did once again its potent fires renew,
Guiding our eyes to find and worship you. . . .

At home the hateful names of parties cease,   25
And factious souls are wearied into peace.
The discontented now are only they
Whose crimes before did your just cause betray :
Of those your edicts some reclaim from sins,
But most your life and blest example wins.   30
Oh happy Prince, whom Heaven hath taught the way
By paying vows to have more vows to pay !
Oh happy age ! Oh times like those alone
By Fate reserved for great Augustus' throne,
When the joint growth of arms and arts foreshow   35
The world a Monarch, and that Monarch *You*.

ANNUS MIRABILIS:

The Year of

WONDERS,
1 6 6 6.

AN HISTORICAL

POEM:

CONTAINING

The Progress and various Successes of our Naval
War with *Holland*, under the Conduct of His
Highness Prince Rupert, and His Grace the
Duke of Albemarl.

And describing

THE FIRE
OF
LONDON.

By John Dryden, Esq;

Multum interest res poscat, an homines latius imperare velint.
Trajan. Imperator. ad Plin.

Urbs antiqua ruit, multos dominata per annos   Virg

London, Printed for *Henry Herringman*, at the *Anchor* in the Lower Walk of the *New Exchange.* 1667.

The Fire of London

(Stanzas 213 to 297, with omissions)

As when some dire usurper Heaven provides
    To scourge his country with a lawless sway,
His birth perhaps some petty village hides
    And sets his cradle out of Fortune's way;

Till, fully ripe, his swelling fate breaks out,   5
    And hurries him to mighty mischiefs on;
His Prince, surprised, at first no ill could doubt,
    And wants the power to meet it when 'tis known.

Such was the rise of this prodigious Fire,
    Which in mean buildings first obscurely bred,   10
From thence did soon to open streets aspire,
    And straight to palaces and temples spread.

The diligence of trades, and noiseful gain,
    And luxury, more late, asleep were laid;
All was the Night's, and in her silent reign   15
    No sound the rest of Nature did invade.

In this deep quiet, from what source unknown,
    Those seeds of fire their fatal birth disclose;
And first, few scattering sparks about were blown,
    Big with the flames that to our ruin rose.   20

Then in some close-pent room it crept along,
    And, smouldering as it went, in silence fed;
Till the infant monster, with devouring strong,
    Walked boldly upright with exalted head.

Now, like some rich or mighty murderer,   25
    Too great for prison, which he breaks with gold,
Who fresher for new mischiefs does appear
    And dares the world to tax him with the old:

So scapes the insulting fire his narrow jail
   And makes small outlets into open air ;   30
There the fierce winds his tender force assail,
   And beat him downward to his first repair.

The winds, like crafty courtesans, withheld
   His flames from burning but to blow them more :
And, every fresh attempt, he is repelled   35
   With faint denials, weaker than before.

And now, no longer letted of his prey,
   He leaps up at it with enraged desire,
O'erlooks the neighbours with a wide survey,
   And nods at every house his threatening fire.   40

The ghosts of traitors from the Bridge descend,
   With bold fanatic spectres to rejoice ;
About the Fire into a dance they bend,
   And sing their sabbath notes with feeble voice. . . .

The Fire meantime walks in a broader gross ;   45
   To either hand his wings he opens wide ;
He wades the streets, and straight he reaches cross,
   And plays his longing flames on the other side.

At first they warm, then scorch, and then they take ;
   Now with long necks from side to side they feed ; 50
At length, grown strong, their mother-fire forsake,
   And a new colony of flames succeed.

To every nobler portion of the town
   The curling billows roll their restless tide ;
In parties now they straggle up and down,   55
   As armies unopposed for prey divide.

One mighty squadron, with a sidewind sped,
   Through narrow lanes his cumbered fire does haste,
By powerful charms of gold and silver led,
   The Lombard bankers and the Change to waste. 60

Another backward to the Tower would go
   And slowly eats his way against the wind ;
But the main body of the marching foe
   Against the imperial palace is designed.

Now day appears, and with the day the King,   65
   Whose early care had robbed him of his rest ;
Far off the cracks of falling houses ring,
   And shrieks of subjects pierce his tender breast. . . .

Himself directs what first is to be done,
   And orders all the succours which they bring ;   70
The helpful and the good about him run,
   And form an army worthy such a King.

He sees the dire contagion spread so fast
   That, where it seizes, all relief is vain,
And therefore must unwillingly lay waste   75
   That country which would else the foe maintain.

The powder blows up all before the Fire ;
   Th' amazed flames stand gather'd on a heap,
And from the precipice's brink retire,
   Afraid to venture on so large a leap.   80

Thus fighting fires a while themselves consume,
   But straight, like Turks, forced on to win or die,
They first lay tender bridges of their fume,
   And o'er the breach in unctuous vapours fly.

Part stays for passage, till a gust of wind   85
   Ships o'er their forces in a shining sheet ;
Part, creeping under ground, their journey blind,
   And, climbing from below, their fellows meet.

Thus to some desert plain, or old wood-side,
   Dire night-hags come from far to dance their round, 90
And o'er broad rivers on their fiends they ride,
   Or sweep in clouds above the blasted ground.

No help avails : for, hydra-like, the Fire
  Lifts up his hundred heads to aim his way ;
And scarce the wealthy can one half retire   95
  Before he rushes in to share the prey. . . .

Night came, but without darkness or repose,
  A dismal picture of the general doom,
Where souls distracted, when the trumpet blows,
  And half unready, with their bodies come.   100

Those who have homes, when home they do repair,
  To a last lodging call their wandering friends ;
Their short uneasy sleeps are broke with care,
  To look how near their own destruction tends.

Those who have none sit round where once it was 105
  And with full eyes each wonted room require,
Haunting the yet warm ashes of the place,
  As murdered men walk where they did expire. . . .

No thought can ease them but their Sovereign's care,
  Whose praise the afflicted as their comfort sing ; 110
Even those whom want might drive to just despair
  Think life a blessing under such a King.

Meantime he sadly suffers in their grief,
  Outweeps an hermit, and outprays a saint ;
All the long night he studies their relief,   115
  How they may be supplied and he may want.

King's prayer.

  ' O God,' said he, ' Thou patron of my days,
  Guide of my youth in exile and distress !
Who me unfriended broughtst by wondrous ways,
  The kingdom of my fathers to possess :   120

  ' Be Thou my judge, with what unwearied care
  I since have laboured for my people's good,
To bind the bruises of a civil war,
  And stop the issues of their wasting blood.

' Thou who hast taught me to forgive the ill   125
    And recompense as friends the good misled,
If mercy be a precept of thy will,
    Return that mercy on thy servant's head.

' Or if my heedless youth has stepped astray,
    Too soon forgetful of thy gracious hand,   130
On me alone thy just displeasure lay,
    But take thy judgements from this mourning land.

' We all have sinned, and Thou hast laid us low
    As humble earth from whence at first we came ;
Like flying shades before the clouds we show,   135
    And shrink like parchment in consuming flame.

' O let it be enough what Thou hast done,
    When spotted deaths ran arm'd through every street,
With poisoned darts, which not the good could shun,
    The speedy could outfly, or valiant meet.   140

' The living few and frequent funerals then
    Proclaimed thy wrath on this forsaken place ;
And now those few, who are returned again,
    Thy searching judgements to their dwellings trace.

' O pass not, Lord, an absolute decree,   145
    Or bind thy sentence unconditional :
But in thy sentence our remorse foresee,
    And in that foresight this thy doom recall.

' Thy threatenings, Lord, as thine Thou mayest revoke :
    But if immutable and fixed they stand,   150
Continue still Thyself to give the stroke,
    And let not foreign foes oppress thy land.'

The Eternal heard, and from the heavenly quire
    Chose out the cherub with the flaming sword,
And bad him swiftly drive the approaching Fire   155
    From where our naval magazines were stored.

.   .   .   .

Nor could thy fabric, Paul's, defend thee long,
  Though thou wert sacred to thy Maker's praise,
Though made immortal by a poet's song,
  And poets' songs the Theban walls could raise.   160

The daring flames peeped in and saw from far
  The awful beauties of the sacred quire ;
But, since it was profaned by civil war,
  Heaven thought it fit to have it purged by fire.

Now down the narrow streets it swiftly came   165
  And, widely opening, did on both sides prey ;
This benefit we sadly owe the flame,
  If only ruin must enlarge our way.

And now four days the Sun had seen our woes,
  Four nights the Moon beheld the incessant Fire ; 170
It seemed as if the stars more sickly rose
  And farther from the feverish North retire.

In the empyrean Heaven, the blessed abode,
  The Thrones and the Dominions prostrate lie,
Not daring to behold their angry God ;   175
  And a hushed silence damps the tuneful sky.

At length the Almighty cast a pitying eye,
  And mercy softly touched his melting breast ;
He saw the town's one half in rubbish lie,
  And eager flames drive on to storm the rest.   180

An hollow crystal pyramid he takes,
  In firmamental waters dipped above ;
Of it a broad extinguisher he makes,
  And hoods the flames that to their quarry strove.

The vanquished fires withdraw from every place,   185
  Or, full with feeding, sink into a sleep :
Each household Genius shows again his face,
  And from the hearths the little Lares creep.

Our King this more than natural change beholds,
  With sober joy his heart and eyes abound ;   190
To the All-good his lifted hands he folds,
  And thanks him low on his redeemed ground.

As when sharp frosts had long constrained the earth,
  A kindly thaw unlocks it with mild rain,
And first the tender blade peeps up to birth,   195
  And straight the green fields laugh with promised grain :

By such degrees the spreading gladness grew
  In every heart, which fear had froze before ;
The standing streets with so much joy they view
  That with less grief the perished they deplore.   200

          .   .   .   .

Methinks already from this chymic flame
  I see a city of more precious mould,
Rich as the town which gives the Indies name,
  With silver paved, and all divine with gold.

Already, labouring with a mighty fate,   205
  She shakes the rubbish from her mounting brow,
And seems to have renewed her charter's date,
  Which Heaven will to the death of Time allow.

More great than human now, and more August,
  New deified she from her Fires does rise :   210
Her widening streets on new foundations trust,
  And, opening, into larger parts she flies.

Before, she like some shepherdess did show,
  Who sate to bathe her by a river's side,
Not answering to her fame, but rude and low,   215
  Nor taught the beauteous arts of modern pride.

Now, like a maiden queen, she will behold
  From her high turrets hourly suitors come ;
The East with incense, and the West with gold,
  Will stand like suppliants to receive her doom.   220

From the D R A M A S

Lines from *The Conquest of Granada*
acted 1670, published 1672

No man has more contempt than I of breath.
But whence hast thou the right to give me death?
Obeyed as sovereign of thy subjects be,
But know that I alone am king of me.
I am as free as nature first made man,   5
Ere the base laws of servitude began,
When wild in woods the noble savage ran.
(Part I, Act I, Scene i.)

True, they have pardoned me; but do they know
What folly 'tis to trust a pardoned foe?
A blush remains in a forgiven face,   10
It wears the silent tokens of disgrace.
Forgiveness to the injured does belong;
But they ne'er pardon who have done the wrong.
(Part II, Act I, Scene ii.)

No; none but I have reason to complain!
So near a kingdom, yet 'tis lost again!   15
O, how unequally in me were joined
A creeping fortune and a soaring mind!
O lottery of fate! where still the wise
Draw blanks of fortune, and the fools the prize!
These cross, ill-shuffled lots from heaven are sent,   20
Yet dull Religion teaches us content;
But when we ask it where that blessing dwells,
It points to pedant colleges, and cells;
There shows it rude, and in a homely dress,
And that proud want mistakes for happiness.   25
(Part II, Act III, Scene ii.)

Love is that madness which all lovers have ;
But yet 'tis sweet and pleasing so to rave :
'Tis an enchantment, where the reason's bound ;
But Paradise is in the enchanted ground ;
A palace, void of envy, cares, and strife,　　　　30
Where gentle hours delude so much of life.
To take those charms away, and set me free,
Is but to send me into misery ;
And prudence, of whose care so much you boast,
Restores those pains which that sweet folly lost.　　35

Fair though you are
As summer mornings, and your eyes more bright
Than stars that twinkle in a winter's night ;
Though you have eloquence to warm and move
Cold age and praying hermits into love ;　　　　40
Though Almahide with scorn rewards my care,—
Yet, than to change, 'tis nobler to despair.
My love's my soul ; and that from Fate is free ;
'Tis that unchanged and deathless part of me.

Ye Gods, why are not hearts first paired above,　　45
But some still interfere in others' love ?
Ere each for each by certain marks are known,
You mould them up in haste, and drop them down ;
And while we seek what carelessly you sort,
You sit in state, and make our pains your sport.　　50
(Part II, Act III, Scene iii.)

'Tis war again, and I am glad 'tis so ;
Success shall now by force and courage go.
Treaties are but the combat of the brain,
Where still the stronger lose, the weaker gain. . . .
The minds of heroes their own measures are,　　55
They stand exempted from the rules of war.

One loose, one sally of the hero's soul
Does all the military art control :
While timorous wit goes round, or fords the shore,
He shoots the gulf, and is already o'er ;　　　　60
And when the enthusiastic fit is spent,
Looks back amazed at what he underwent.

(Part II, Act IV, Scene ii.)

Lines from *Aureng-zebe*

acted 1675, published 1676

WHEN I consider Life, 'tis all a cheat ;
Yet, fooled with hope, men favour the deceit ;
Trust on, and think to-morrow will repay :
To-morrow 's falser than the former day ;
Lies worse ; and while it says, we shall be blest　　5
With some new joys, cuts off what we possesst.
Strange cozenage ! None would live past years again,
Yet all hope pleasure in what yet remain ;
And, from the dregs of Life, think to receive
What the first sprightly running could not give.　　10
I'm tired with waiting for this chemic gold,
Which fools us young, and beggars us when old.

(Act IV, Scene i.)

Prologue to *Aureng-zebe*

OUR author by experience finds it true,
'Tis much more hard to please himself than you ;
And, out of no feign'd modesty, this day
Damns his laborious trifle of a play ;
Not that it's worse than what before he writ,   5
But he has now another taste of wit ;
And, to confess a truth, though out of time,
Grows weary of his long-loved mistress, Rhyme.
Passion's too fierce to be in fetters bound,
And Nature flies him like enchanted ground :   10
What verse can do he has performed in this,
Which he presumes the most correct of his ;
But spite of all his pride, a secret shame
Invades his breast at Shakespeare's sacred name :
Awed when he hears his godlike Romans rage,   15
He in a just despair would quit the stage ;
And to an age less polished, more unskilled,
Does with disdain the foremost honours yield.
As with the greater dead he dares not strive,
He would not match his verse with those who live :   20
Let him retire, betwixt two ages cast,
The first of this, and hindmost of the last. . . .

All for Love

acted and published 1678

From Act I

Enter ANTONY, *walking with a disturbed motion before he speaks.*

Antony. They tell me, 'tis my birthday, and I'll keep it
With double pomp of sadness.
'Tis what the day deserves, which gave me breath.
Why was I raised the meteor of the world,
Hung in the skies, and blazing as I travelled,   5
Till all my fires were spent ; and then cast downward
To be trod out by Caesar ?

   Ventidius [*aside*].   On my soul,
'Tis mournful, wondrous mournful !

   Ant.   Count thy gains.   10
Now, Antony, wouldst thou be born for this ?
Glutton of fortune, thy devouring youth
Has starved thy wanting age.

   Vent.   How sorrow shakes him !   [*Aside.*
So, now the tempest tears him up by the roots,   15
And on the ground extends the noble ruin.

            [ANTONY *having thrown himself down.*

Lie there, thou shadow of an emperor ;
The place thou pressest on thy mother earth
Is all thy empire now : now it contains thee ;
Some few days hence, and then 'twill be too large,   20
When thou'rt contracted in thy narrow urn,
Shrunk to a few cold ashes ; then Octavia
(For Cleopatra will not live to see it),
Octavia then will have thee all her own,
And bear thee in her widowed hand to Caesar ;   25
Caesar will weep, the crocodile will weep,

To see his rival of the universe
Lie still and peaceful there. I'll think no more on't.

    Ant. Give me some music : look that it be sad :
I'll soothe my melancholy, till I swell,   30
And burst myself with sighing.—   [*Soft music.*
'Tis somewhat to my humour. Stay, I fancy
I'm now turned wild, a commoner of nature ;
Of all forsaken, and forsaking all ;
Live in a shady forest's sylvan scene,   35
Stretched at my length beneath some blasted oak,
I lean my head upon the mossy bark,
And look just of a piece, as I grew from it ;
My uncombed locks, matted like mistletoe,
Hang o'er my hoary face ; a murm'ring brook   40
Runs at my foot.

    Vent. Methinks I fancy
Myself there too.

    Ant. The herd come jumping by me,
And, fearless, quench their thirst, while I look on,   45
And take me for their fellow-citizen.
More of this image, more ; it lulls my thoughts.

                  [*Soft music again.*

    Vent. I must disturb him ; I can hold no longer.

                  [*Stands before him.*

    Ant. [*starting up*]. Art thou Ventidius ?

    Vent. Are you Antony ?   50
I'm liker what I was, than you to him
I left you last.

    Ant. I'm angry.

    Vent. So am I.

    Ant. I would be private : leave me.   55

    Vent. Sir, I love you,
And therefore will not leave you.

    Ant. Will not leave me ?
Where have you learnt that answer ? Who am I ?

Vent. My emperor ; the man I love next Heaven : 60
If I said more, I think 'twere scarce a sin :
You're all that 's good, and god-like.

   Ant. All that 's wretched.
You will not leave me then ?

   Vent. 'Twas too presuming   65
To say I would not ; but I dare not leave you :
And, 'tis unkind in you to chide me hence
So soon, when I so far have come to see you.

   Ant. Now thou hast seen me, art thou satisfied ?
For, if a friend, thou hast beheld enough ;   70
And, if a foe, too much.

   Vent. [*weeping*]. Look, emperor, this is no common dew.
I have not wept this forty year ; but now
My mother comes afresh into my eyes ;
I cannot help her softness.   75

   Ant. By heaven, he weeps ! poor good old man, he
     weeps !
The big round drops course one another down
The furrows of his cheeks. Stop 'em, Ventidius,
Or I shall blush to death : they set my shame,
That caused 'em, full before me.   80

   Vent. I'll do my best.

   Ant. Sure there 's contagion in the tears of friends :
See, I have caught it too. Believe me, 'tis not
For my own griefs, but thine.—Nay, father !

   Vent. Emperor.   85

   Ant. Emperor ! Why, that 's the style of victory ;
The conqu'ring soldier, red with unfelt wounds,
Salutes his general so : but never more
Shall that sound reach my ears.

   Vent. I warrant you.   90

   Ant. Actium, Actium ! Oh !——

   Vent. It sits too near you.

   Ant. Here, here it lies ; a lump of lead by day,

And, in my short, distracted, nightly slumbers,
The hag that rides my dreams.——   95
   Vent.   Out with it ; give it vent.
   Ant.   Urge not my shame.
I lost a battle.
   Vent.   So has Julius done.
   Ant.   Thou favour'st me, and speak'st not half thou
   think'st ;   100
For Julius fought it out, and lost it fairly :
But Antony——
   Vent.   Nay, stop not.
   Ant.   Antony,—
Well, thou wilt have it,—like a coward, fled,   105
Fled while his soldiers fought ; fled first, Ventidius.
Thou long'st to curse me, and I give thee leave.
I know thou cam'st prepared to rail.
   Vent.   I did.
   Ant.   I'll help thee.—I have been a man, Ventidius.
   Vent.   Yes, and a brave one ; but——   111
   Ant.   I know thy meaning.
But I have lost my reason, have disgraced
The name of soldier, with inglorious ease.
In the full vintage of my flowing honours,   115
Sat still, and saw it prest by other hands.
Fortune came smiling to my youth, and wooed it,
And purple greatness met my ripened years.
When first I came to empire, I was borne
On tides of people, crowding to my triumphs ;   120
The wish of nations ; and the willing world
Received me as its pledge of future peace ;
I was so great, so happy, so beloved,
Fate could not ruin me ; till I took pains
And worked against my fortune, chid her from me, 125
And turned her loose ; yet still she came again.
My careless days, and my luxurious nights,

At length have wearied her, and now she 's gone,
Gone, gone, divorced for ever. Help me, soldier,
To curse this madman, this industrious fool,   130
Who laboured to be wretched : pr'ythee curse me.
   Vent. No.
   Ant. Why ?
   Vent. You are too sensible already
Of what you've done, too conscious of your failings ; 135
And like a scorpion, whipt by others first
To fury, sting yourself in mad revenge.
I would bring balm, and pour it in your wounds,
Cure your distempered mind, and heal your fortunes.
   Ant. I know thou would'st.   140
   Vent. I will.
   Ant. Ha, ha, ha, ha !
   Vent. You laugh.
   Ant. I do, to see officious love
Give cordials to the dead.   145
   Vent. You would be lost, then ?
   Ant. I am.
   Vent. I say, you are not. Try your fortune.
   Ant. I have, to the utmost. Dost thou think me
    desperate,
Without just cause ? No, when I found all lost   150
Beyond repair, I hid me from the world,
And learnt to scorn it here ; which now I do
So heartily, I think it is not worth
The cost of keeping.
   Vent. Caesar thinks not so ;   155
He'll thank you for the gift he could not take.
You would be killed, like Tully, would you ? do,
Hold out your throat to Caesar, and die tamely.
   Ant. No, I can kill myself ; and so resolve.
   Vent. I can die with you too, when time shall serve ;
But Fortune calls upon us now to live,   161

To fight, to conquer.

   Ant. Sure thou dream'st, Ventidius.

   Vent. No ; 'tis you dream ; you sleep away your hours

In desperate sloth, miscalled philosophy.   165

Up, up, for honour's sake ; twelve legions wait you,

And long to call you chief : By painful journeys

I led them, patient, both of heat and hunger,

Down from the Parthian marches, to the Nile.

'Twill do you good to see their sunburnt faces,   170

Their scarred cheeks, and chopt hands : there 's virtue in 'em.

They'll sell those mangled limbs at dearer rates

Than yon trim bands can buy.

   Ant. Where left you them ?

   Vent. I said in Lower Syria.   175

   Ant. Bring 'em hither ;

There may be life in these.

   Vent. They will not come.

   Ant. Why didst thou mock my hopes with promised aids,

To double my despair ? They're mutinous.   180

   Vent. Most firm and loyal.

   Ant. Yet they will not march

To succour me. O trifler !

   Vent. They petition

You would make haste to head 'em.   185

   Ant. I'm besieged.

   Vent. There 's but one way shut up : How came I hither ?

   Ant. I will not stir.

   Vent. They would perhaps desire

A better reason.   190

   Ant. I have never used

My soldiers to demand a reason of

My actions. Why did they refuse to march ?
  Vent. They said they would not fight for Cleopatra.
  Ant. What was't they said ?   195
  Vent. They said they would not fight for Cleopatra.
Why should they fight indeed, to make her conquer,
And make you more a slave ?   to gain you kingdoms,
Which, for a kiss, at your next midnight feast,
You'll sell to her ?   Then she new-names her jewels, 200
And calls this diamond such or such a tax ;
Each pendant in her ear shall be a province.
  Ant. Ventidius, I allow your tongue free licence
On all my other faults ; but, on your life,
No word of Cleopatra : she deserves   205
More worlds than I can lose.
  Vent. Behold, you Powers,
To whom you have intrusted humankind !
See Europe, Afric, Asia, put in balance,
And all weighed down by one light, worthless woman !
I think the gods are Antonies, and give,   211
Like prodigals, this nether world away
To none but wasteful hands.
  Ant. You grow presumptuous.
  Vent. I take the privilege of plain love to speak. 215
  Ant. Plain love ! plain arrogance, plain insolence '
Thy men are cowards ; thou, an envious traitor ;
Who, under seeming honesty, hast vented
The burden of thy rank, o'erflowing gall.
O that thou wert my equal ; great in arms   220
As the first Caesar was, that I might kill thee
Without a stain to honour !
  Vent. You may kill me ;
You have done more already,—called me traitor.
  Ant. Art thou not one ?   225
  Vent. For showing you yourself,
Which none else durst have done ? but had I been

That name, which I disdain to speak again,
I needed not have sought your abject fortunes,
Come to partake your fate, to die with you.   230
What hindered me to have led my conquering eagles
To fill Octavius' bands ?   I could have been
A traitor then, a glorious, happy traitor,
And not have been so called.

    Ant. Forgive me, soldier ;   235
I've been too passionate.

    Vent. You thought me false ;
Thought my old age betrayed you : Kill me, sir ;
Pray kill me ; yet you need not, your unkindness
Has left your sword no work.   240

    Ant. I did not think so ;
I said it in my rage : Pr'ythee forgive me.
Why didst thou tempt my anger, by discovery
Of what I would not hear ?

    Vent. No prince but you   245
Could merit that sincerity I used,
Nor durst another man have ventured it ;
But you, ere love misled your wandering eyes,
Were sure the chief and best of human race,
Framed in the very pride and boast of Nature ;   250
So perfect, that the gods who formed you wondered
At their own skill, and cried—A lucky hit
Has mended our design.   Their envy hindered,
Else you had been immortal, and a pattern,
When Heaven would work for ostentation sake   255
To copy out again.

    Ant. But Cleopatra—
Go on ; for I can bear it now.

    Vent. No more.

    Ant. Thou dar'st not trust my passion ; but thou
    may'st :   260
Thou only lov'st ; the rest have flattered me.

Vent.   Heaven's blessing on your heart for that kind
    word !
May I believe you love me ?   Speak again.
   Ant.   Indeed I do.   Speak this, and this, and this.
                                 [*Hugging him.*
Thy praises were unjust ; but, I'll deserve them,   265
And yet mend all.   Do with me what thou wilt ;
Lead me to victory ! thou know'st the way.
   Vent.   And, will you leave this——
   Ant.   Pr'ythee do not curse her,
And I will leave her ; though, Heaven knows, I love 270
Beyond life, conquest, empire, all ; but honour :
But I will leave her.
   Vent.   That 's my royal master.
And, shall we fight ?
   Ant.   I warrant thee, old soldier.   275
Thou shalt behold me once again in iron,
And at the head of our old troops, that beat
The Parthians, cry aloud—Come follow me !
   Vent.   Oh, now I hear my emperor ! in that word
Octavius fell.   Gods, let me see that day,   280
And, if I have ten years behind, take all ;
I'll thank you for the exchange.
   Ant.   O Cleopatra !
   Vent.   Again ?
   Ant.   I've done : in that last sigh, she went.   285
Caesar shall know what 'tis to force a lover
From all he holds most dear.
   Vent.   Methinks, you breathe
Another soul : Your looks are more divine ;
You speak a hero, and you move a god.   290
   Ant.   Oh, thou hast fired me ; my soul 's up in arms,
And mans each part about me : Once again,
That noble eagerness of fight has seized me ;
That eagerness with which I darted upward

To Cassius' camp : In vain the steepy hill   295
Opposed my way ; in vain a war of spears
Sung round my head, and planted on my shield :
I won the trenches, while my foremost men
Lagged on the plain below.

   Vent. Ye Gods, ye Gods,   300
For such another hour !

   Ant. Come on, my soldier !
Our hearts and arms are still the same : I long
Once more to meet our foes ; that thou and I,
Like Time and Death, marching before our troops,   305
May taste fate to 'em ; mow 'em out a passage,
And, entering where the foremost squadrons yield,
Begin the noble harvest of the field.   [*Exeunt.*

From A c t I V

Men are but children of a larger growth ;
Our appetites as apt to change as theirs,
And full as craving too, and full as vain ;
And yet the soul, shut up in her dark room,
Viewing so clear abroad, at home sees nothing ;
But like a mole in earth, busy and blind,
Works all her folly up, and casts it outward
To the world's open view.

ABSALOM

AND

ACHITOPHEL.

A

POEM.

--------Si Propiùs ſtes
Te Capiet Magis--------

LONDON,

Printed for *J. T.* and are to be Sold by *W. Davis* in
Amen-Corner, 1 68 1.

F

ABSALOM and ACHITOPHEL

Published 17 November 1681

In pious times, ere priestcraft did begin,
Before polygamy was made a sin,
When man on many multiplied his kind,
Ere one to one was cursedly confined,
When nature prompted and no law denied   5
Promiscuous use of concubine and bride,
Then Israel's monarch after Heaven's own heart
His vigorous warmth did variously impart
To wives and slaves, and, wide as his command,
Scattered his Maker's image through the land.   10
Michal, of royal blood, the crown did wear,
A soil ungrateful to the tiller's care :
Not so the rest ; for several mothers bore
To godlike David several sons before.
But since like slaves his bed they did ascend,   15
No true succession could their seed attend.
Of all this numerous progeny was none
So beautiful, so brave, as Absalon :
Whether, inspired by some diviner lust,
His father got him with a greater gust,   20
Or that his conscious destiny made way
By manly beauty to imperial sway.
Early in foreign fields he won renown
With kings and states allied to Israel's crown ;
In peace the thoughts of war he could remove   25
And seemed as he were only born for love.
Whate'er he did was done with so much ease,
In him alone 'twas natural to please ;
His motions all accompanied with grace,

And Paradise was opened in his face. 30
With secret joy indulgent David viewed
His youthful image in his son renewed ;
To all his wishes nothing he denied
And made the charming Annabel his bride.
What faults he had (for who from faults is free ?) 35
His father could not or he would not see.
Some warm excesses, which the law forbore,
Were construed youth, that purged by boiling o'er ;
And Amnon's murder, by a specious name
Was called a just revenge for injured fame. 40
Thus praised, and loved, the noble youth remained,
While David undisturbed in Sion reigned.
But life can never be sincerely blest ;
Heaven punishes the bad, and proves the best.
The Jews, a headstrong, moody, murmuring race 45
As ever tried the extent and stretch of grace ;
God's pampered people, whom, debauched with ease,
No king could govern nor no God could please ;
(Gods they had tried of every shape and size
That godsmiths could produce or priests devise :) 50
These Adam-wits, too fortunately free,
Began to dream they wanted liberty ;
And when no rule, no precedent was found
Of men by laws less circumscribed and bound,
They led their wild desires to woods and caves, 55
And thought that all but savages were slaves.
They who, when Saul was dead, without a blow
Made foolish Ishbosheth the crown forego ;
Who banished David did from Hebron bring,
And with a general shout proclaimed him King ; 60
Those very Jews who at their very best
Their humour more than loyalty exprest,
Now wondered why so long they had obeyed
An idol monarch which their hands had made ;

F 2

Thought they might ruin him they could create,   65
Or melt him to that golden calf, a State.
But these were random bolts ; no formed design
Nor interest made the factious crowd to join :
The sober part of Israel, free from stain,
Well knew the value of a peaceful reign ;   70
And, looking backward with a wise affright,
Saw seams of wounds dishonest to the sight,
In contemplation of whose ugly scars
They cursed the memory of civil wars.
The moderate sort of men, thus qualified,   75
Inclined the balance to the better side ;
And David's mildness managed it so well,
The bad found no occasion to rebel.
But, when to sin our biassed nature leans,
The careful Devil is still at hand with means,   80
And providently pimps for ill desires ;
The good old cause, revived, a plot requires.
Plots, true or false, are necessary things,
To raise up commonwealths and ruin kings.

.   .   .   .

This plot, which failed for want of common sense,   134
Had yet a deep and dangerous consequence ;
For as, when raging fevers boil the blood,
The standing lake soon floats into a flood,
And every hostile humour which before
Slept quiet in its channels bubbles o'er ;
So several factions from this first ferment   140
Work up to foam, and threat the government.
Some by their friends, more by themselves thought wise,
Opposed the power to which they could not rise.
Some had in courts been great and, thrown from thence,
Like fiends were hardened in impenitence.   145
Some, by their Monarch's fatal mercy grown,
From pardoned rebels, kinsmen to the throne,

Were raised in power and public office high ;
Strong bands, if bands ungrateful men could tie.
Of these the false Achitophel was first,   150
A name to all succeeding ages curst :
For close designs and crooked counsels fit,
Sagacious, bold, and turbulent of wit,
Restless, unfixed in principles and place,
In power unpleased, impatient of disgrace ;   155
A fiery soul, which, working out its way,
Fretted the pigmy body to decay,
And o'er-informed the tenement of clay.
A daring pilot in extremity,
Pleased with the danger, when the waves went high   160
He sought the storms ; but, for a calm unfit,
Would steer too nigh the sands to boast his wit.
Great wits are sure to madness near allied
And thin partitions do their bounds divide ;
Else, why should he, with wealth and honour blest,   165
Refuse his age the needful hours of rest ?
Punish a body which he could not please,
Bankrupt of life, yet prodigal of ease ?
And all to leave what with his toil he won
To that unfeathered two-legged thing, a son,   170
Got, while his soul did huddled notions try,
And born a shapeless lump, like anarchy.
In friendship false, implacable in hate,
Resolved to ruin or to rule the state ;
To compass this the triple bond he broke,   175
The pillars of the public safety shook,
And fitted Israel for a foreign yoke ;
Then, seized with fear, yet still affecting fame,
Usurped a patriot's all-atoning name.
So easy still it proves in factious times   180
With public zeal to cancel private crimes.
How safe is treason and how sacred ill,

Where none can sin against the people's will,
Where crowds can wink, and no offence be known,
Since in another's guilt they find their own.   185
Yet, fame deserved, no enemy can grudge ;
The statesman we abhor, but praise the judge.
In Israel's courts ne'er sat an Abbethdin
With more discerning eyes or hands more clean,
Unbribed, unsought, the wretched to redress,   190
Swift of dispatch and easy of access.
Oh, had he been content to serve the crown
With virtues only proper to the gown,
Or had the rankness of the soil been freed
From cockle that oppressed the noble seed,   195
David for him his tuneful harp had strung,
And Heaven had wanted one immortal song.
But wild ambition loves to slide, not stand,
And fortune's ice prefers to virtue's land.
Achitophel, grown weary to possess   200
A lawful fame and lazy happiness,
Disdained the golden fruit to gather free
And lent the crowd his arm to shake the tree.
Now, manifest of crimes contrived long since,
He stood at bold defiance with his Prince,   205
Held up the buckler of the people's cause
Against the crown, and skulked behind the laws.
The wished occasion of the Plot he takes ;
Some circumstances finds, but more he makes ;
By buzzing emissaries fills the ears   210
Of listening crowds with jealousies and fears
Of arbitrary counsels brought to light,
And proves the King himself a Jebusite.
Weak arguments ! which yet he knew full well
Were strong with people easy to rebel.   215
For governed by the moon, the giddy Jews
Tread the same track when she the prime renews :

And once in twenty years, their scribes record,
By natural instinct they change their lord.
Achitophel still wants a chief, and none   220
Was found so fit as warlike Absalon.
Not that he wished his greatness to create,
(For politicians neither love nor hate :)
But, for he knew his title not allowed
Would keep him still depending on the crowd,   225
That kingly power, thus ebbing out, might be
Drawn to the dregs of a democracy.
Him he attempts with studied arts to please
And sheds his venom in such words as these :

  ' Auspicious Prince ! at whose nativity   230
Some royal planet ruled the southern sky ;
Thy longing country's darling and desire,
Their cloudy pillar, and their guardian fire,
Their second Moses, whose extended wand
Divides the seas and shows the promised land,   235
Whose dawning day in every distant age
Has exercised the sacred prophet's rage,
The people's prayer, the glad diviner's theme,
The young men's vision, and the old men's dream !
Thee, Saviour, thee, the nation's vows confess,   240
And, never satisfied with seeing, bless :
Swift unbespoken pomps thy steps proclaim,
And stammering babes are taught to lisp thy name.
How long wilt thou the general joy detain,
Starve and defraud the people of thy reign ?   245
Content ingloriously to pass thy days,
Like one of virtue's fools that feeds on praise ;
Till thy fresh glories, which now shine so bright,
Grow stale and tarnish with our daily sight.
Believe me, royal youth, thy fruit must be   250
Or gathered ripe, or rot upon the tree.

Heaven has to all allotted, soon or late,
Some lucky revolution of their fate :
Whose motions if we watch and guide with skill,
(For human good depends on human will,)   255
Our fortune rolls as from a smooth descent
And from the first impression takes the bent ;
But, if unseized, she glides away like wind,
And leaves repenting folly far behind.
Now, now she meets you with a glorious prize   260
And spreads her locks before her as she flies.
Had thus old David, from whose loins you spring,
Not dared, when fortune called him to be King,
At Gath an exile he might still remain,
And Heaven's anointing oil had been in vain.   265
Let his successful youth your hopes engage,
But shun the example of declining age.
Behold him setting in his western skies,
The shadows lengthening as the vapours rise.
He is not now, as when, on Jordan's sand,   270
The joyful people thronged to see him land,
Covering the beach and blackening all the strand ;
But like the Prince of Angels, from his height
Comes tumbling downward with diminished light. . . .
All sorts of men, by my successful arts   289
Abhorring kings, estrange their altered hearts
From David's rule : and 'tis the general cry,
Religion, commonwealth, and liberty.
If you, as champion of the public good,
Add to their arms a chief of royal blood,
What may not Israel hope, and what applause   295
Might such a general gain by such a cause !
Not barren praise alone, that gaudy flower
Fair only to the sight, but solid power ;
And nobler is a limited command,
Given by the love of all your native land,   300

Than a successive title, long and dark,
Drawn from the mouldy rolls of Noah's ark.'

   .   .   .   .

  He said, and this advice above the rest   477
With Absalom's mild nature suited best ;
Unblamed of life (ambition set aside),
Not stained with cruelty, nor puffed with pride.   480
How happy had he been, if Destiny
Had higher placed his birth, or not so high !
His kingly virtues might have claimed a throne
And blessed all other countries but his own ;
But charming greatness since so few refuse,   485
'Tis juster to lament him than accuse.
Strong were his hopes a rival to remove,
With blandishments to gain the public love,
To head the faction while their zeal was hot,
And popularly prosecute the plot.   490
To further this, Achitophel unites
The malcontents of all the Israelites,
Whose differing parties he could wisely join
For several ends to serve the same design :
The best, and of the princes some were such,   495
Who thought the power of monarchy too much ;
Mistaken men, and patriots in their hearts,
Not wicked, but seduced by impious arts.
By these the springs of property were bent,
And wound so high they cracked the government.   500
The next for interest sought to embroil the state,
To sell their duty at a dearer rate,
And make their Jewish markets of the throne,
Pretending public good to serve their own.
Others thought kings an useless heavy load,   505
Who cost too much and did too little good.
These were for laying honest David by
On principles of pure good husbandry.

With them joined all the haranguers of the throng
That thought to get preferment by the tongue. . . .   510
But far more numerous was the herd of such   533
Who think too little and who talk too much.
These, out of mere instinct, they knew not why,
Adored their fathers' God and property,
And by the same blind benefit of Fate
The Devil and the Jebusite did hate :
Born to be saved, even in their own despite,
Because they could not help believing right.   540
Such were the tools ; but a whole Hydra more
Remains of sprouting heads too long to score.
Some of their chiefs were princes of the land :
In the first rank of these did Zimri stand :
A man so various, that he seemed to be   545
Not one, but all mankind's epitome.
Stiff in opinions, always in the wrong,
Was everything by starts, and nothing long ;
But in the course of one revolving moon
Was chymist, fiddler, statesman, and buffoon ;   550
Then all for women, painting, rhyming, drinking,
Besides ten thousand freaks that died in thinking.
Blest madman, who could every hour employ
With something new to wish, or to enjoy !
Railing and praising were his usual themes,   555
And both, to show his judgment, in extremes :
So over violent, or over civil,
That every man with him was God or Devil.
In squandering wealth was his peculiar art ;
Nothing went unrewarded but desert.   560
Beggared by fools, whom still he found too late,
He had his jest, and they had his estate.
He laughed himself from Court ; then sought relief
By forming parties, but could ne'er be chief :
For, spite of him, the weight of business fell   565

On Absalom and wise Achitophel ;
Thus wicked but in will, of means bereft,
He left not faction, but of that was left.

. . . .

Surrounded thus with friends of every sort,   682
Deluded Absalom forsakes the court ;
Impatient of high hopes, urged with renown,
And fired with near possession of a crown.   685
The admiring crowd are dazzled with surprise,
And on his goodly person feed their eyes :
His joy concealed, he sets himself to show,
On each side bowing popularly low :
His looks, his gestures, and his words he frames,   690
And with familiar ease repeats their names.
Thus formed by nature, furnished out with arts,
He glides unfelt into their secret hearts. . . .

Youth, beauty, graceful action, seldom fail,   723
But common interest always will prevail ;
And pity never ceases to be shown
To him who makes the people's wrongs his own.
The crowd, that still believe their kings oppress,
With lifted hands their young Messiah bless :
Who now begins his progress to ordain
With chariots, horsemen, and a numerous train ;   730
From east to west his glories he displays,
And, like the sun, the promised land surveys.
Fame runs before him as the morning star,
And shouts of joy salute him from afar ;
Each house receives him as a guardian god,   735
And consecrates the place of his abode.

. . . .

Now what relief can righteous David bring ?   811
How fatal 'tis to be too good a king !
Friends he has few, so high the madness grows ;
Who dare be such, must be the people's foes.

Yet some there were, even in the worst of days ;   815
Some let me name, and naming is to praise.

In this short file Barzillai first appears,
Barzillai, crowned with honour and with years :
Long since, the rising rebels he withstood
In regions waste, beyond the Jordan's flood :   820
Unfortunately brave to buoy the state,
But sinking underneath his master's fate.
In exile with his godlike prince he mourned,
For him he suffered, and with him returned.
The court he practised, not the courtier's art :   825
Large was his wealth, but larger was his heart,
Which well the noblest objects knew to chuse,
The fighting warrior, and recording Muse. . . .
Next them a train of loyal peers ascend ;   876
Sharp-judging Adriel, the Muses' friend,
Himself a Muse : in Sanhedrin's debate
True to his Prince, but not a slave of state ;
Whom David's love with honours did adorn   880
That from his disobedient son were torn.
Jotham of piercing wit and pregnant thought,
Endued by nature and by learning taught
To move assemblies, who but only tried
The worse a while, then chose the better side ;   885
Nor chose alone, but turned the balance too,
So much the weight of one brave man can do.
Hushai, the friend of David in distress,
In public storms of manly stedfastness ;
By foreign treaties he informed his youth,   890
And joined experience to his native truth.
His frugal care supplied the wanting throne,
Frugal for that, but bounteous of his own :
'Tis easy conduct when exchequers flow,
But hard the task to manage well the low.   895

For sovereign power is too depressed or high,
When kings are forced to sell, or crowds to buy.
Indulge one labour more, my weary Muse,
For Amiel ; who can Amiel's praise refuse ?
Of ancient race by birth, but nobler yet   900
In his own worth, and without title great :
The Sanhedrin long time as chief he ruled,
Their reason guided, and their passion cooled ;
So dexterous was he in the Crown's defence,
So formed to speak a loyal nation's sense,   905
That, as their band was Israel's tribes in small,
So fit was he to represent them all.
Now rasher charioteers the seat ascend,
Whose loose careers his steady skill commend :
They, like the unequal ruler of the day,   910
Misguide the seasons, and mistake the way ;
While he, withdrawn, at their mad labour smiles,
And safe enjoys the sabbath of his toils. . . .

  With all these loads of injuries opprest,   933
And long revolving in his careful breast
The event of things, at last his patience tired,
Thus from his royal throne, by Heaven inspired,
The godlike David spoke ; with awful fear
His train their Maker in their master hear.

  ' Thus long have I, by native mercy swayed,
My wrongs dissembled, my revenge delayed ;   940
So willing to forgive the offending age ;
So much the father did the king assuage.
But now so far my clemency they slight,
The offenders question my forgiving right.
That one was made for many, they contend ;   945
But 'tis to rule, for that 's a monarch's end.
They call my tenderness of blood my fear,

Though manly tempers can the longest bear.
Yet, since they will divert my native course,
'Tis time to show I am not good by force.   950
Those heaped affronts that haughty subjects bring
Are burdens for a camel, not a king.
Kings are the public pillars of the State,
Born to sustain and prop the nation's weight :
If my young Samson will pretend a call   955
To shake the column, let him share the fall ;
But oh that yet he would repent and live !
How easy 'tis for parents to forgive !
With how few tears a pardon might be won
From nature, pleading for a darling son !   960
Poor pitied youth, by my paternal care
Raised up to all the height his frame could bear !
Had God ordained his fate for empire born,
He would have given his soul another turn :
Gulled with a patriot's name, whose modern sense   965
Is one that would by law supplant his prince :
The people's brave, the politician's tool ;
Never was patriot yet but was a fool.
Whence comes it that religion and the laws
Should more be Absalom's than David's cause ?   970
His old instructor, ere he lost his place,
Was never thought endued with so much grace.
Good heavens, how faction can a patriot paint !
My rebel ever proves my people's saint.
Would *they* impose an heir upon the throne ?   975
Let Sanhedrins be taught to give their own.
A king 's at least a part of government,
And mine as requisite as their consent :
Without my leave a future king to choose
Infers a right the present to depose.   980
True, they petition me to approve their choice :
But Esau's hands suit ill with Jacob's voice.

My pious subjects for my safety pray,
Which to secure they take my power away.
From plots and treasons Heaven preserve my years,   985
But save me most from my petitioners.
Unsatiate as the barren womb or grave ;
God cannot grant so much as they can crave.
What then is left but with a jealous eye
To guard the small remains of royalty ?   990
The law shall still direct my peaceful sway,
And the same law teach rebels to obey :
Votes shall no more established power control,
Such votes as make a part exceed the whole :
No groundless clamours shall my friends remove,   995
Nor crowds have power to punish ere they prove ;
For gods, and godlike kings their care express
Still to defend their servants in distress.
Oh that my power to saving were confined !
Why am I forced, like Heaven, against my mind   1000
To make examples of another kind ?
Must I at length the sword of justice draw ?
Oh curst effects of necessary law !
How ill my fear they by my mercy scan !
Beware the fury of a patient man.   1005
Law they require, let Law then show her face. . . .
   He said.   The Almighty, nodding, gave consent ;   1026
And peals of thunder shook the firmament.
Henceforth a series of new time began,
The mighty years in long procession ran :
Once more the godlike David was restored,   1030
And willing nations knew their lawful lord.

From

THE MEDAL

A Satire against Sedition

Published middle of March 1682

POWER was his aim; but, thrown from that pretence,　50
The wretch turned loyal in his own defence,
And malice reconciled him to his prince.
Him in the anguish of his soul he served,
Rewarded faster still than he deserved.
Behold him, now exalted into trust;　　　　　55
His counsels oft convenient, seldom just;
Even in the most sincere advice he gave
He had a grudging still to be a knave.
The frauds he learnt in his fanatic years
Made him uneasy in his lawful gears.　　　　60
At best as little honest as he could:
And, like white witches, mischievously good.
To his first bias, longingly he leans;
And *rather* would be great by wicked means.

　.　　.　　.　　.　　.　　.　　.　　.

When his just sovereign by no impious way　77
Could be seduced to arbitrary sway,
Forsaken of that hope, he shifts his sail;
Drives down the current with a popular gale;　80
And shows the fiend confessed without a veil.
He preaches to the crowd that power is lent,
But not conveyed to kingly government;
That claims successive bear no binding force;
That coronation oaths are things of course;　85
Maintains the multitude can never err;
And sets the people in the papal chair.

The reason's obvious ; *interest never lies ;*
The most have still their interest in their eyes ;
The power is always theirs, and power is ever wise.   90
Almighty crowd, thou shortenest all dispute ;
Power is thy essence ; wit thy attribute !
Nor faith nor reason make thee at a stay,
Thou leapst o'er all eternal truths in thy Pindaric way !
Athens, no doubt, did righteously decide,   95
When Phocion and when Socrates were tried ;
As righteously they did those dooms repent ;
Still they were wise, whatever way they went.
Crowds err not, though to both extremes they run ;
To kill the father and recall the son.   100
Some think the fools were most as times went then,
But now the world's o'erstocked with prudent men.
The common cry is even religion's test ;
The Turk's is, at Constantinople, best,
Idols in India, Popery at Rome,   105
And our own worship only true at home,
And true, but for the time, 'tis hard to know
How long we please it shall continue so ;
This side to-day, and that to-morrow burns ;
So all are God almighties in their turns.   110
A tempting doctrine, plausible and new ;
What fools our fathers were, if this be true !
Who, to destroy the seeds of civil war,
Inherent right in monarchs did declare :
And, that a lawful power might never cease,   115
Secured succession, to secure our peace.

.   .   .   .
Such impious axioms foolishly they show ;   246
For in some soils republics will not grow :
Our temperate isle will no extremes sustain
Of popular sway or arbitrary reign :
But slides between them both into the best ;   250
Secure in freedom, in a monarch blest.

M A C   F L E C K N O E

Published before October 1682

The opening lines

ALL human things are subject to decay,
And, when Fate summons, monarchs must obey :
This Flecknoe found, who, like Augustus, young
Was called to Empire and had governed long :
In prose and verse was owned, without dispute   5
Through all the realms of nonsense, absolute.
This aged Prince now flourishing in peace,
And blest with issue of a large increase,
Worn out with business, did at length debate
To settle the succession of the State ;   10
And pondering which of all his sons was fit
To reign, and wage immortal war with wit,
Cried, 'tis resolved ; for Nature pleads that he
Should only rule, who most resembles me :
Shadwell alone my perfect image bears,   15
Mature in dulness from his tender years ;
Shadwell alone of all my sons is he
Who stands confirmed in full stupidity.
The rest to some faint meaning make pretence,
But Shadwell never deviates into sense.   20
Some beams of wit on other souls may fall,
Strike through and make a lucid interval ;
But Shadwell's genuine night admits no ray,
His rising fogs prevail upon the day . . .

From *The Second Part* of

ABSALOM AND ACHITOPHEL

Published 10 November, 1682

Og and Doeg.

.   .   .   .

And hasten Og and Doeg to rehearse,
Two fools that crutch their feeble sense on verse,
Who by my muse to all succeeding times   410
Shall live in spite of their own dogrel rhymes.
   Doeg, though without knowing how or why,
Made still a blundering kind of melody ;
Spurred boldly on, and dashed through thick and thin,
Through sense and nonsense, never out nor in ;   415
Free from all meaning, whether good or bad,
And in one word, heroically mad.
He was too warm on picking work to dwell,
But faggoted his notions as they fell,
And, if they rhymed and rattled, all was well.   420

.   .   .   .

With all this bulk there 's nothing lost in Og,   462
For every inch that is not fool is rogue . . .
Doeg, whom God for mankind's mirth has made,   492
O'ertops thy talent in thy very trade ;
Doeg to thee, thy paintings are so coarse,
A poet is, though he 's the poet's horse.   495
A double noose thou on thy neck dost pull
For writing treason and for writing dull . . .
I will not rake the dunghill of thy crimes,   504
For who would read thy life that reads thy rhymes ?
But of king David's foes be this the doom,
May all be like the young man Absalom ;
And for my foes may this their blessing be,
To talk like Doeg and to write like thee.

RELIGIO LAICI

OR A

Laymans Faith.

A

P O E M.

Written by Mr. *D R Y D E N.*

Ornari res ipfa negat; contenta doceri.

L O N D O N,

Printed for *Jacob Tonfon* at the *Judge's Head* in *Chancery-lane,* near *Fleet-ftreet.* 1682.

RELIGIO LAICI

Published end of November 1682

DIM as the borrowed beams of moon and stars
To lonely, weary, wandering travellers
Is Reason to the soul : and as on high
Those rolling fires discover but the sky,
Not light us here ; so Reason's glimmering ray⎫   5
Was lent, not to assure our doubtful way,   ⎬
But guide us upward to a better day.   ⎭
And as those nightly tapers disappear
When day's bright lord ascends our hemisphere,
So pale grows Reason at Religion's sight,   10
So dies, and so dissolves in supernatural light.
Some few, whose lamp shone brighter, have been led
From cause to cause to Nature's secret head,
And found that one first principle must be ;
But what or who that UNIVERSAL HE ;   15
Whether some soul encompassing this ball,
Unmade, unmoved, yet making, moving All,
Or various atoms' interfering dance
Leapt into form (the noble work of chance,)
Or this great All was from eternity,   ⎫   20
Not even the Stagirite himself could see,   ⎬
And Epicurus guessed as well as he.   ⎭
As blindly groped they for a future state,
As rashly judged of Providence and Fate.
But least of all could their endeavours find   25
What most concerned the good of human kind ;
For Happiness was never to be found,
But vanished from them like enchanted ground.
One thought Content the good to be enjoyed ;
This every little accident destroyed.   30

The wiser madmen did for Virtue toil,
A thorny, or at best a barren soil ;
In pleasure some their glutton souls would steep,
But found their line too short, the well too deep,
And leaky vessels which no bliss could keep.   35
Thus anxious thoughts in endless circles roll,
Without a centre where to fix the soul.
In this wild maze their vain endeavours end :
How can the less the greater comprehend ?
Or finite Reason reach Infinity ?   40
For what could fathom GOD were more than He.

.   .   .   .

Shall I speak plain, and in a nation free   316
Assume an honest layman's liberty ?
I think, according to my little skill,
To my own mother Church submitting still,
That many have been saved, and many may,   320
Who never heard this question brought in play.
The unlettered Christian, who believes in gross,
Plods on to Heaven and ne'er is at a loss ;
For the strait gate would be made straiter yet,
Were none admitted there but men of wit.   325
The few by Nature formed, with learning fraught,
Born to instruct, as others to be taught,
Must study well the sacred page ; and see
Which doctrine, this or that, does best agree
With the whole tenour of the work divine,   330
And plainliest points to Heaven's revealed design ;
Which exposition flows from genuine sense,
And which is forced by wit and eloquence.
Not that tradition's parts are useless here,
When general, old, disinteressed, and clear :   335
That ancient fathers thus expound the page
Gives truth the reverend majesty of age,
Confirms its force by biding every test,

For best authorities, next rules, are best ;
And still the nearer to the spring we go,   340
More limpid, more unsoiled, the waters flow.
Thus, first traditions were a proof alone,
Could we be certain such they were, so known :
But since some flaws in long descent may be,
They make not truth but probability.   345
Even Arius and Pelagius durst provoke
To what the centuries preceding spoke.
Such difference is there in an oft-told tale,
But truth by its own sinews will prevail.
Tradition written, therefore, more commends   350
Authority than what from voice descends :
And this, as perfect as its kind can be,
Rolls down to us the sacred history :
Which, from the Universal Church received,
Is tried, and after for its self believed.   355
    The partial Papists would infer from hence,
Their Church in last resort should judge the sense.
But first they would assume with wondrous art
Themselves to be the whole, who are but part
Of that vast frame, the Church ; yet grant they were
The handers down, can they from thence infer   361
A right to interpret ? or would they alone
Who brought the present claim it for their own ?
The Book 's a common largess to mankind,
Not more for them than every man designed ;   365
The welcome news is in the letter found ;
The carrier 's not commissioned to expound.
It speaks its self, and what it does contain
In all things needful to be known is plain.
    In times o'ergrown with rust and ignorance   370
A gainful trade their clergy did advance ;
When want of learning kept the laymen low
And none but priests were authorized to know ;

When what small knowledge was in them did dwell,
And he a God who could but read or spell ;   375
Then Mother Church did mightily prevail ;
She parcelled out the Bible by retail,
But still expounded what she sold or gave,
To keep it in her power to damn and save.
Scripture was scarce, and as the market went,   380
Poor laymen took salvation on content,
As needy men take money, good or bad ;
God's word they had not, but the priest's they had.
Yet, whate'er false conveyances they made,
The lawyer still was certain to be paid.   385
In those dark times they learned their knack so well,
That by long use they grew infallible.
At last, a knowing age began to enquire
If they the Book, or that did them inspire ;
And, making narrower search, they found, though late,
That what they thought the priest's was their estate, 391
Taught by the will produced, the written word,
How long they had been cheated on record.
Then every man who saw the title fair
Claimed a child's part, and put in for a share,   395
Consulted soberly his private good,
And saved himself as cheap as e'er he could.
   'Tis true, my friend (and far be flattery hence),
This good had full as bad a consequence ;
The Book thus put in every vulgar hand,   400
Which each presumed he best could understand,
The common rule was made the common prey,
And at the mercy of the rabble lay.
The tender page with horny fists was galled,
And he was gifted most that loudest bawled ;   405
The spirit gave the doctoral degree,
And every member of a Company
Was of his trade and of the Bible free.

Plain truths enough for needful use they found,
But men would still be itching to expound ;   410
Each was ambitious of the obscurest place,
No measure taken from Knowledge, all from Grace.
Study and pains were now no more their care ;
Texts were explained by fasting and by prayer :
This was the fruit the private spirit brought,   415
Occasioned by great zeal and little thought.
While crowds unlearned, with rude devotion warm,
About the sacred viands buzz and swarm,
The fly-blown text creates a crawling brood,
And turns to maggots what was meant for food.   420
A thousand daily sects rise up, and die ;
A thousand more the perished race supply :
So all we make of Heaven's discovered will
Is not to have it, or to use it ill.
The danger 's much the same, on several shelves   425
If others wreck us or we wreck ourselves.
   What then remains but, waving each extreme,
The tides of ignorance and pride to stem ?
Neither so rich a treasure to forgo,
Nor proudly seek beyond our power to know ?   430
Faith is not built on disquisitions vain ;
The things we must believe are few and plain :
But since men will believe more than they need,
And every man will make himself a creed,
In doubtful questions 'tis the safest way   435
To learn what unsuspected ancients say ;
For 'tis not likely we should higher soar
In search of Heaven than all the Church before ;
Nor can we be deceived, unless we see
The Scripture and the Fathers disagree.   440
If after all they stand suspected still,
(For no man's faith depends upon his will,)
'Tis some relief, that points not clearly known

Without much hazard may be let alone ;
And after hearing what our Church can say,   445
If still our reason runs another way,
That private reason 'tis more just to curb
Than by disputes the public peace disturb.
For points obscure are of small use to learn :
But common quiet is mankind's concern.   450

    Thus have I made my own opinions clear,
Yet neither praise expect nor censure fear ;
And this unpolished, rugged verse I chose
As fittest for discourse, and nearest prose ;
For while from sacred truth I do not swerve,   455
Tom Sternhold's or Tom Shadwell's rhymes will serve.

To   the   Memory   of
Mr. Oldham

Printed in the *Remains* of John Oldham, 1684

FAREWELL, too little and too lately known,
Whom I began to think and call my own ;
For sure our souls were near allied ; and thine
Cast in the same poetic mould with mine.
One common note on either lyre did strike,   5
And knaves and fools we both abhorred alike :
To the same goal did both our studies drive,
The last set out the soonest did arrive.
Thus Nisus fell upon the slippery place,
While his young friend performed and won the race. 10
O early ripe ! to thy abundant store
What could advancing age have added more ?
It might (what Nature never gives the young)
Have taught the numbers of thy native tongue.

But satire needs not those, and wit will shine 15
Through the harsh cadence of a rugged line.
A noble error, and but seldom made,
When poets are by too much force betrayed.
Thy generous fruits, though gathered ere their prime,
Still showed a quickness ; and maturing time 20
But mellows what we write to the dull sweets of rhyme.
Once more, hail and farewell ; farewell, thou young,
But ah too short, Marcellus of our tongue ;
Thy brows with ivy and with laurels bound ;
But Fate and gloomy night encompass thee around. 25

The Twenty-Ninth Ode

Of the Third Book of Horace

Paraphrased in Pindaric Verse

Printed in *Sylvae*, 1685

(Lines 50–87)

ENJOY the present smiling hour ;
And put it out of Fortune's power :
The tide of business, like the running stream,
Is sometimes high, and sometimes low,
A quiet ebb, or a tempestuous flow, 5
And always in extreme.
Now with a noiseless gentle course
It keeps within the middle bed ;
Anon it lifts aloft the head,
And bears down all before it, with impetuous force : 10
And trunks of trees come rolling down,
Sheep and their folds together drown :
Both house and homestead into seas are borne ;

And rocks are from their old foundations torn,
And woods, made thin with winds, their scattered honours
        mourn.   15

   Happy the man, and happy he alone,
     He, who can call to-day his own :
     He, who, secure within, can say,
   To-morrow do thy worst, for I have lived to-day.
     Be fair, or foul, or rain, or shine,   20
   The joys I have possessed, in spite of fate, are mine.
   Not Heaven itself upon the past has power ;
But what has been, has been, and I have had my hour.

    Fortune, that with malicious joy
      Does man her slave oppress,   25
    Proud of her office to destroy,
      Is seldom pleased to bless :
    Still various, and unconstant still,
   But with an inclination to be ill ;
    Promotes, degrades, delights in strife,   30
    And makes a lottery of life.
    I can enjoy her while she 's kind ;
    But when she dances in the wind,
    And shakes the wings, and will not stay,
    I puff the prostitute away :   35
The little or the much she gave, is quietly resigned :
   Content with poverty, my soul I arm ;
   And Virtue, though in rags, will keep me warm.

To the Pious Memory

Of the Accomplist Young L A D Y

Mrs Anne Killigrew,

Excellent in the two Sister-Arts of Poësie, and Painting.

An O D E

Printed in *Poems by Mrs Anne Killigrew*, 1686; published
end of 1685.

I

THOU youngest virgin-daughter of the skies,
Made in the last promotion of the blest ;
  Whose palms, new plucked from paradise,
In spreading branches more sublimely rise,
Rich with immortal green above the rest :   5
Whether, adopted to some neighbouring star,
Thou roll'st above us, in thy wandering race ;
Or, in procession fixed and regular,
  Moved with the heaven's majestic pace,
  Or, called to more superior bliss,   10
Thou treadest, with Seraphims, the vast abyss :
Whatever happy region is thy place,
Cease thy celestial song a little space ;
(Thou wilt have time enough for hymns divine,
  Since Heaven's eternal year is thine.)   15
Hear then a mortal muse thy praise rehearse,
       In no ignoble verse ;
But such as thy own voice did practise here,
When thy first fruits of poesy were given,
To make thyself a welcome inmate there ;   20
    While yet a young probationer,
      And candidate of Heaven.

2

If by traduction came thy mind,
    Our wonder is the less to find
A soul so charming from a stock so good ;   25
Thy father was transfused into thy blood :
So wert thou born into the tuneful strain,
(An early, rich, and inexhausted vein.)
    But if thy pre-existing soul
    Was formed, at first, with myriads more,   30
It did through all the mighty poets roll,
    Who Greek or Latin laurels wore,
And was that Sappho last, which once it was before.
    If so, then cease thy flight, O heaven-born mind !
    Thou hast no dross to purge from thy rich ore :   35
Nor can thy soul a fairer mansion find
Than was the beauteous frame she left behind :
Return, to fill or mend the quire of thy celestial kind.

3

May we presume to say, that at thy birth,
New joy was sprung in Heaven, as well as here on earth ?
    For sure the milder planets did combine   41
    On thy auspicious horoscope to shine,
And even the most malicious were in trine.
    Thy brother-angels at thy birth
    Strung each his lyre, and tuned it high,   45
    That all the people of the sky
Might know a poetess was born on earth.
    And then if ever, mortal ears
    Had heard the music of the spheres !
    And if no clustering swarm of bees   50
On thy sweet mouth distilled their golden dew,
    'Twas that such vulgar miracles
    Heaven had not leisure to renew :
For all the blest fraternity of love
Solemnized there thy birth, and kept thy holiday above.

4

O gracious God! How far have we 56
Prophaned thy heavenly gift of poesy?
Made prostitute and profligate the Muse,
Debased to each obscene and impious use,
Whose harmony was first ordained above 60
For tongues of angels, and for hymns of love?
O wretched we! why were we hurried down
   This lubric and adulterate age,
(Nay, added fat pollutions of our own)
To increase the steaming ordures of the stage? 65
What can we say to excuse our second fall?
Let this thy vestal, Heaven, atone for all!
Her Arethusian stream remains unsoiled,
Unmixed with foreign filth, and undefiled,
Her wit was more than man, her innocence a child! 70

5

Art she had none, yet wanted none,
   For Nature did that want supply:
So rich in treasures of her own,
   She might our boasted stores defy:
Such noble vigour did her verse adorn, 75
That it seemed borrowed, where 'twas only born.
Her morals too were in her bosom bred
   By great examples daily fed,
What in the best of books, her father's life, she read.
And to be read herself she need not fear; 80
Each test, and every light, her Muse will bear,
Though Epictetus with his lamp were there.
Even love (for love sometimes her Muse expressed)
Was but a lambent flame which played about her breast:
   Light as the vapours of a morning dream, 85
So cold herself, whilst she such warmth expressed,
   'Twas Cupid bathing in Diana's stream.

.   .   .   .

8

Now all those charms, that blooming grace,   149
The well-proportioned shape, and beauteous face,
Shall never more be seen by mortal eyes ;
In earth the much lamented virgin lies !
Nor wit, nor piety could Fate prevent ;
Nor was the cruel Destiny content
To finish all the murder at a blow,   155
To sweep at once her life and beauty too ;
But, like a hardened felon, took a pride
   To work more mischievously slow,
   And plundered first, and then destroyed.
O double sacrilege on things divine,   160
To rob the relic, and deface the shrine !
    But thus Orinda died :
Heaven, by the same disease, did both translate,
As equal were their souls, so equal was their fate.

9

Meantime her warlike brother on the seas   165
His waving streamers to the winds displays,
And vows for his return, with vain devotion, pays.
   Ah, generous youth, that wish forbear,
   The winds too soon will waft thee here !
   Slack all thy sails, and fear to come,   170
Alas, thou know'st not, thou art wrecked at home !
No more shalt thou behold thy sister's face,
Thou hast already had her last embrace.
But look aloft, and if thou ken'st from far,
Among the Pleiads, a new-kindled star,   175
If any sparkles, than the rest, more bright,
'Tis she that shines in that propitious light.

10

When in mid-air the golden trump shall sound,
  To raise the nations under ground ;
When in the valley of Jehosaphat   180
The judging God shall close the book of Fate ;
  And there the last assizes keep,
  For those who wake, and those who sleep ;
  When rattling bones together fly
  From the four corners of the sky,   185
When sinews o'er the skeletons are spread,
Those clothed with flesh, and life inspires the dead ;
The sacred poets first shall hear the sound,
  And foremost from the tomb shall bound :
For they are covered with the lightest ground ;   190
And straight, with inborn vigour, on the wing,
Like mounting larks, to the new morning sing.
There thou, sweet saint, before the quire shalt go,
As harbinger of Heaven, the way to show,
The way which thou so well hast learned below.   195

THE

HIND

AND THE

PANTHER.

A

POEM,

In Three Parts.

———*Antiquam exquirite matrem.*
Et vera, inceſſu, patuit Dea.——— ⎫ Virg. -
⎭

LONDON,
Printed for *Jacob Tonſon*, at the *Judges Head* in
Chancery Lane near *Fleetſtreet*, 1687.

The Hind; the Panther

(I, 1–8, 25–34, 327–34)

A MILK-WHITE Hind, immortal and unchanged,
Fed on the lawns and in the forest ranged ;
Without unspotted, innocent within,
She feared no danger, for she knew no sin.
Yet had she oft been chased with horns and hounds   5
And Scythian shafts, and many winged wounds
Aimed at her heart ; was often forced to fly,
And doomed to death, though fated not to die. . . .

   Panting and pensive now she ranged alone,
And wandered in the kingdoms once her own.   10
The common hunt, though from their rage restrained
By sovereign power, her company disdained,
Grinned as they passed, and with a glaring eye
Gave gloomy signs of secret enmity.
'Tis true she bounded by, and tripped so light,   15
They had not time to take a steady sight ;
For truth has such a face and such a mien
As to be loved needs only to be seen.

     .   .   .   .

   The Panther, sure the noblest next the Hind,
And fairest creature of the spotted kind :   20
Oh, could her inborn stains be washed away,
She were too good to be a beast of prey !
How can I praise, or blame, and not offend,
Or how divide the frailty from the friend ?
Her faults and virtues lie so mixed, that she   25
Nor wholly stands condemned nor wholly free.

Belief

(I, 62–92; 141–7)

What weight of ancient witness can prevail,
If private reason hold the public scale ?
But, gracious God, how well dost Thou provide
For erring judgements an unerring guide !
Thy throne is darkness in the abyss of light,   5
A blaze of glory that forbids the sight :
O teach me to believe Thee thus concealed,
And search no farther than Thyself revealed :
But her alone for my director take
Whom Thou hast promised never to forsake !   10
My thoughtless youth was winged with vain desires,
My manhood, long misled by wandering fires,
Followed false lights ; and when their glimpse was gone
My pride struck out new sparkles of her own.
Such was I, such by nature still I am ;   15
Be Thine the glory and be mine the shame !
Good life be now my task ; my doubts are done ;
(What more could fright my faith than Three in One ?)
Can I believe eternal God could lie
Disguised in mortal mould and infancy?   20
That the great Maker of the world could die ?
And, after that, trust my imperfect sense
Which calls in question his omnipotence ?
Can I my reason to my faith compel,
And shall my sight, and touch, and taste rebel ?   25
Superior faculties are set aside :
Shall their subservient organs be my guide ?
Then let the moon usurp the rule of day,
And winking tapers show the sun his way ;
For what my senses can themselves perceive   30
I need no revelation to believe. . .

To take up half on trust, and half to try,
Name it not faith, but bungling bigotry.
Both knave and fool the merchant we may call
To pay great sums and to compound the small,   35
For who would break with Heaven, and would not break
  for all ?
Rest then, my soul, from endless anguish freed ;
Nor sciences thy guide, nor sense thy creed.
Faith is the best ensurer of thy bliss.

Conversion

(III, 279–97)

Be vengeance wholly left to powers divine,
And let Heaven judge betwixt your sons and mine :
If joys hereafter must be purchased here
With loss of all that mortals hold so dear,
Then welcome infamy and public shame,   5
And, last, a long farewell to worldly fame.
'Tis said with ease, but oh, how hardly tried
By haughty souls to human honour tied !
O sharp convulsive pangs of agonizing pride !
Down then, thou rebel, never more to rise ;   10
And what thou didst and dost so dearly prize,
That fame, that darling fame, make that thy sacrifice.
'Tis nothing thou hast given ; then add thy tears
For a long race of unrepenting years :
'Tis nothing yet ; yet all thou hast to give :   15
Then add those *may-be* years thou hast to live.
Yet nothing still : then poor and naked come,
Thy Father will receive his unthrift home,
And thy blest Saviour's blood discharge the mighty sum.

The Fable of the Swallows

(III, 427–460 ; 561–638)

The Swallow, privileged above the rest
Of all the birds as man's familiar guest,
Pursues the sun in summer, brisk and bold,
But wisely shuns the persecuting cold ;
Is well to chancels and to chimneys known,   5
Though 'tis not thought she feeds on smoke alone.
From hence she has been held of heavenly line,
Endued with particles of soul divine.
This merry chorister had long possessed
Her summer seat, and feathered well her nest ;   10
Till frowning skies began to change their cheer,
And time turned up the wrong side of the year ;
The shedding trees began the ground to strow
With yellow leaves, and bitter blasts to blow.
Sad auguries of winter thence she drew,   15
Which by instinct, or prophecy, she knew :
When prudence warned her to remove betimes,
And seek a better heaven and warmer climes.

Her sons were summoned on a steeple's height,
And, called in common council, vote a flight ;   20
The day was named, the next that should be fair ;
All to the general rendezvous repair,
They try their fluttering wings and trust themselves in air.
But whether upward to the moon they go,
Or dream the winter out in caves below,   25
Or hawk at flies elsewhere, concerns not us to know.

Southwards, you may be sure, they bent their flight,
And harboured in a hollow rock at night ;
Next morn they rose, and set up every sail ;
The wind was fair, but blew a mackrel gale :   30

The sickly young sat shivering on the shore,
Abhorred salt-water never seen before,
And prayed their tender mothers to delay
The passage, and expect a fairer day.

 . . . .

 No longer doubting, all prepare to fly   35
And repossess their patrimonial sky.
The priest before them did his wings display ;
And that good omens might attend their way,
As luck would have it, 'twas St. Martin's day.
 Who but the Swallow now triumphs alone ? 40
The canopy of heaven is all her own ;
Her youthful offspring to their haunts repair,
And glide along in glades, and skim in air,
And dip for insects in the purling springs,
And stoop on rivers to refresh their wings. . . . 45
 And now 'twas time (so fast their numbers rise)
To plant abroad, and people colonies.
The youth drawn forth, as Martin had desired
(For so their cruel destiny required),   65
Were sent far off on an ill-fated day ;
The rest would need conduct them on their way,
And Martin went, because he feared alone to stay.
 So long they flew with inconsiderate haste,
That now their afternoon began to waste ; 70
And, what was ominous, that very morn
The sun was entered into Capricorn ;
Which, by their bad astronomers' account,
That week the Virgin balance should remount.
An infant moon eclipsed him in his way, 75
And hid the small remainders of his day.
The crowd amazed pursued no certain mark ;
But birds met birds, and justled in the dark ;
Few mind the public in a panic fright ;
And fear increased the horror of the night. 80

Night came, but unattended with repose ;
Alone she came, no sleep their eyes to close,
Alone, and black she came ; no friendly stars arose.
   What should they do, beset with dangers round,
No neighbouring dorp, no lodging to be found,   85
But bleaky plains, and bare unhospitable ground ?
The latter brood, who just began to fly,
Sick-feathered and unpractised in the sky,
For succour to their helpless mother call :
She spread her wings ; some few beneath them crawl ; 90
She spread them wider yet, but could not cover all.
To augment their woes, the winds began to move
Debate in air for empty fields above,
Till Boreas got the skies, and poured amain
His rattling hailstones mixed with snow and rain.   95
   The joyless morning late arose, and found
A dreadful desolation reign around,
Some buried in the snow, some frozen to the ground.
The rest were struggling still with death, and lay
The Crows' and Ravens' rights, an undefended prey ; 100
Excepting Martin's race ; for they and he
Had gained the shelter of a hollow tree :
But soon discovered by a sturdy clown,
He headed all the rabble of a town,
And finished them with bats, or poled them down.   105
Martin himself was caught alive, and tried
For treasonous crimes, because the laws provide
No Martin there in winter shall abide.
High on an oak which never leaf shall bear,
He breathed his last, exposed to open air ;   110
And there his corpse, unblessed, is hanging still,
To show the change of winds with his prophetic bill.

James II

(III, 906–29)

A plain good man, whose name is understood,
(So few deserve the name of plain and good)
Of three fair lineal lordships stood possessed,
And lived, as reason was, upon the best.
Inured to hardships from his early youth,   5
Much had he done and suffered for his truth :
At land, and sea, in many a doubtful fight,
Was never known a more adventurous knight,
Who oftener drew his sword, and always for the right.
  As Fortune would (his fortune came though late   10
He took possession of his just estate ;
Nor racked his tenants with increase of rent,
Nor lived too sparing, nor too largely spent ;
But overlooked his hinds ; their pay was just
And ready, for he scorned to go on trust :   15
Slow to resolve, but in performance quick ;
So true, that he was awkward at a trick.
For little souls on little shifts rely,
And coward arts of mean expedients try :
The noble mind will dare do anything but lie.   20
False friends (his deadliest foes) could find no way
But shows of honest bluntness, to betray ;
That unsuspected plainness he believed ;
He looked into himself, and was deceived.

A SONG for
St. Cecilia's Day

NOVEMBER 22, 1687

I

FROM harmony, from heavenly harmony
  This universal frame began ;
  When Nature underneath a heap
    Of jarring atoms lay,
    And could not heave her head,   5
  The tuneful voice was heard from high,
    Arise, ye more than dead.
  Then cold and hot and moist and dry
  In order to their stations leap,
    And MUSIC's power obey.   10
From harmony, from heavenly harmony
  This universal frame began :
  From harmony to harmony
Through all the compass of the notes it ran,
The diapason closing full in man.   15

2

What passion cannot MUSIC raise and quell ?
  When Jubal struck the chorded shell,
  His listening brethren stood around,
  And, wondering, on their faces fell
  To worship that celestial sound :   20
Less than a god they thought there could not dwell
  Within the hollow of that shell,
  That spoke so sweetly, and so well.
What passion cannot MUSIC raise and quell ?

3

The TRUMPETS loud clangor 25
    Excites us to arms
With shrill notes of anger
    And mortal alarms.
  The double double double beat
    Of the thundering DRUM 30
    Cries, hark ! the foes come ;
Charge, charge, 'tis too late to retreat.

4

The soft complaining FLUTE
In dying notes discovers
The woes of hopeless lovers, 35
Whose dirge is whispered by the warbling LUTE.

5

Sharp VIOLINS proclaim
Their jealous pangs and desperation,
Fury, frantic indignation,
Depth of pains and height of passion, 40
    For the fair, disdainful dame.

6

But oh ! what art can teach,
What human voice can reach
The sacred ORGAN's praise ?
Notes inspiring holy love, 45
Notes that wing their heavenly ways
    To mend the choirs above.

7

Orpheus could lead the savage race,
And trees unrooted left their place,
    Sequacious of the lyre ; 50
But bright CECILIA raised the wonder higher :
When to her organ vocal breath was given,
  An angel heard, and straight appeared
    Mistaking earth for Heaven.

GRAND CHORUS

As from the power of sacred lays   55
*   The spheres began to move,*
And sung the great Creator's praise
*   To all the blessed above ;*
So, when the last and dreadful hour
This crumbling pageant shall devour,   60
The TRUMPET shall be heard on high,
The dead shall live, the living die,
And MUSIC shall untune the sky.

Lines printed under the Engraved Portrait of Milton

In Tonson's edition of ' Paradise Lost ', 1688

THREE poets, in three distant ages born,
Greece, Italy, and England did adorn.
The first in loftiness of thought surpassed,
The next in majesty, in both the last :
The force of Nature could no farther go ;   5
To make a third she joined the former two.

VENI, CREATOR SPIRITUS

Translated in Paraphrase

Printed in *Examen Poeticum*, 1693

CREATOR Spirit, by whose aid
The world's foundations first were laid,
Come, visit every pious mind ;
Come, pour thy joys on human kind ;
From sin, and sorrow set us free ;   5
And make thy temples worthy Thee.

O, source of uncreated light,
The Father's promised Paraclete !
Thrice holy Fount, thrice holy Fire,
Our hearts with heavenly love inspire ;   10
Come, and thy sacred unction bring
To sanctify us, while we sing !

Plenteous of grace, descend from high,
Rich in thy sevenfold energy !
Thou strength of his almighty hand,   15
Whose power does heaven and earth command :
Proceeding Spirit, our defence,
Who dost the gift of tongues dispense,
And crown'st thy gift with eloquence !

Refine and purge our earthy parts ;   20
But, oh, inflame and fire our hearts !
Our frailties help, our vice control ;
Submit the senses to the soul ;
And when rebellious they are grown,
Then, lay thy hand, and hold them down.   25

Chase from our minds the infernal foe ;
And peace, the fruit of love, bestow ;
And, lest our feet should step astray,
Protect and guide us in the way.

Make us eternal truths receive,   30
And practise all that we believe :
Give us Thyself, that we may see
The Father and the Son, by Thee.

Immortal honour, endless fame,
Attend the Almighty Father's name :   35
The Saviour Son be glorified,
Who for lost man's redemption died :
And equal adoration be,
Eternal Paraclete, to Thee.

To my Dear Friend

Mr. Congreve

On His COMEDY, call'd,

The Double-Dealer

Printed in the first edition of *The Double-Dealer*, 1694

WELL then, the promised hour is come at last ;
The present age of wit obscures the past :
Strong were our sires, and as they fought they writ,
Conquering with force of arms and dint of wit ;
Theirs was the giant race before the flood ;   5
And thus, when Charles returned, our empire stood.
Like Janus he the stubborn soil manured,
With rules of husbandry the rankness cured :
Tamed us to manners, when the stage was rude ;
And boistrous English wit with art endued.   10
Our age was cultivated thus at length ;
But what we gained in skill we lost in strength ;
Our builders were, with want of genius, curst ;
The second temple was not like the first :
Till you, the best Vitruvius, come at length,   15
Our beauties equal, but excel our strength.
Firm Doric pillars found your solid base ;
The fair Corinthian crowns the higher space ;
Thus all below is strength, and all above is grace.
In easy dialogue is Fletcher's praise :   20
He moved the mind, but had no power to raise.
Great Jonson did by strength of judgement please :
Yet, doubling Fletcher's force, he wants his ease.
In differing talents both adorned their age,
One for the study, t' other for the stage.   25

But both to Congreve justly shall submit,
One matched in judgement, both o'er-matched in wit.
In him all beauties of this age we see,
Etherege his courtship, Southern's purity,
The satire, wit, and strength of manly Wycherly.   30
All this in blooming youth you have achieved ;
Nor are your foiled contemporaries grieved ;
So much the sweetness of your manners move,
We cannot envy you because we love.
Fabius might joy in Scipio, when he saw   35
A beardless consul made against the law,
And join his suffrage to the votes of Rome,
Though he with Hannibal was overcome.
Thus old Romano bowed to Raphael's fame,
And scholar to the youth he taught, became.   40
  Oh that your brows my laurel had sustained,
Well had I been deposed, if you had reigned !
The father had descended for the son ;
For only you are lineal to the throne.
Thus, when the state one Edward did depose,   45
A greater Edward in his room arose.
But now, not I, but poetry is curst ;
For Tom the Second reigns like Tom the First.
But let them not mistake my patron's part,
Nor call his charity their own desert.   50
Yet this I prophesy ; thou shalt be seen
(Though with some short parenthesis between)
High on the throne of wit ; and, seated there,
Not mine (that 's little) but thy laurel wear.
Thy first attempt an early promise made ;   55
That early promise this has more than paid.
So bold, yet so judiciously you dare,
That your least praise, is to be regular.
Time, place, and action, may with pains be wrought,
But genius must be born, and never can be taught.   60

This is your portion, this your native store ; }
Heaven, that but once was prodigal before,
To Shakespeare gave as much ; she could not give him
    more.

  Maintain your post : that 's all the fame you need ;
For 'tis impossible you should proceed.   65
Already I am worn with cares and age,
And just abandoning the ungrateful stage :
Unprofitably kept at Heaven's expense,
I live a rent-charge on his providence :
But you, whom every muse and grace adorn,   70
Whom I foresee to better fortune born,
Be kind to my remains ; and oh defend,
Against your judgment, your departed friend !
Let not the insulting foe my fame pursue ;
But shade those laurels which descend to you :   75
And take for tribute what these lines express :
You merit more ; nor could my love do less.

From the Translation of

The TENTH SATIRE of Juvenal

1693

Look round the habitable world, how few
Know their own good ; or knowing it, pursue.
How void of reason are our hopes and fears !
What in the conduct of our life appears
So well designed, so luckily begun,
But, when we have our wish, we wish undone ?

ALEXANDER'S FEAST,

or the Power of Music

An ODE
IN HONOUR OF ST. CECILIA'S DAY

NOVEMBER 22, 1697

I

'TWAS at the royal feast, for Persia won,
   By Philip's warlike son :
  Aloft in awful state
  The godlike hero sate
   On his imperial throne :   5
 His valiant peers were placed around ;
Their brows with roses and with myrtles bound.
 (So should desert in arms be crowned :)
The lovely Thais by his side,
Sat like a blooming eastern bride   10
In flower of youth and beauty's pride.
  Happy, happy, happy pair !
   None but the brave,
   None but the brave,
 None but the brave deserves the fair.   15

CHORUS

Happy, happy, happy pair !
 None but the brave,
 None but the brave,
None but the brave deserves the fair.

II

 Timotheus placed on high   20
 Amid the tuneful quire,
With flying fingers touched the lyre :
The trembling notes ascend the sky,
 And heavenly joys inspire.

The song began from Jove,   25
  Who left his blissful seats above,
  (Such is the power of mighty love.)
A dragon's fiery form belied the god :
  Sublime on radiant spires he rode,
  When he to fair Olympia pressed :   30
  And while he sought her snowy breast :
  Then, round her slender waist he curled,
And stamped an image of himself, a sovereign of the world.
  The listening crowd admire the lofty sound,
  A present deity, they shout around :   35
  A present deity, the vaulted roofs rebound.
        With ravished ears
        The monarch hears,
        Assumes the god,
        Affects to nod,   40
     And seems to shake the spheres.

CHORUS

With ravished ears
The monarch hears,
Assumes the god,
Affects to nod,   45
And seems to shake the spheres.

III

The praise of Bacchus then the sweet musician sung,
  Of Bacchus ever fair, and ever young :
    The jolly god in triumph comes ;
    Sound the trumpets, beat the drums ;   50
      Flushed with a purple grace
      He shows his honest face :
Now give the hautboys breath ; he comes, he comes.
    Bacchus, ever fair and young,
      Drinking joys did first ordain ;   55
    Bacchus blessings are a treasure ;
    Drinking is the soldier's pleasure ;

Rich the treasure,
Sweet the pleasure,
Sweet is pleasure after pain.   60

CHORUS

Bacchus blessings are a treasure ;
Drinking is the soldier's pleasure ;
   Rich the treasure,
   Sweet the pleasure,
Sweet is pleasure after pain.   65

IV

Soothed with the sound the king grew vain ;
Fought all his battles o'er again ;
And thrice he routed all his foes, and thrice he slew the slain.
   The master saw the madness rise,
   His glowing cheeks, his ardent eyes ;   70
   And while he heaven and earth defied,
   Changed his hand, and checked his pride.
      He chose a mournful muse,
      Soft pity to infuse ;
   He sung Darius great and good,   75
      By too severe a fate,
   Fallen, fallen, fallen, fallen,
   Fallen from his high estate,
      And weltring in his blood :
   Deserted at his utmost need   80
   By those his former bounty fed ;
   On the bare earth exposed he lies,
   With not a friend to close his eyes.
With downcast looks the joyless victor sate,
      Revolving in his altered soul   85
         The various turns of chance below ;
      And, now and then, a sigh he stole,
         And tears began to flow.

CHORUS

Revolving in his altered soul
The various turns of chance below ; 90
And, now and then, a sigh he stole,
And tears began to flow.

V

The mighty master smiled to see
That love was in the next degree ;
'Twas but a kindred sound to move, 95
For pity melts the mind to love.
  Softly sweet, in Lydian measures,
  Soon he soothed his soul to pleasures.
  War, he sung, is toil and trouble ;
  Honour but an empty bubble. 100
    Never ending, still beginning,
    Fighting still, and still destroying,
      If the world be worth thy winning,
      Think, O think, it worth enjoying.
        Lovely Thais sits beside thee, 105
        Take the good the gods provide thee.
The many rend the skies with loud applause ;
So love was crowned, but music won the cause.
  The prince, unable to conceal his pain,
        Gazed on the fair 110
        Who caused his care,
  And sighed and looked, sighed and looked,
  Sighed and looked, and sighed again :
At length, with love and wine at once oppressed,
The vanquished victor sunk upon her breast. 115

CHORUS

The prince, unable to conceal his pain,
    Gazed on the fair
    Who caused his care,

And sighed and looked, sighed and looked,
Sighed and looked, and sighed again :   120
At length, with love and wine at once oppressed,
The vanquished victor sunk upon her breast.

VI

Now strike the golden lyre again :
A louder yet, and yet a louder strain.
  Break his bands of sleep asunder,   125
And rouse him, like a rattling peal of thunder.
    Hark, hark, the horrid sound
      Has raised up his head ;
      As awaked from the dead,
    And amazed, he stares around.   130
  Revenge, revenge, Timotheus cries,
      See the furies arise !
    See the snakes that they rear,
    How they hiss in their hair,
  And the sparkles that flash from their eyes !   135
      Behold a ghastly band,
      Each a torch in his hand !
Those are Grecian ghosts, that in battle were slain,
        And unburied remain
        Inglorious on the plain.   140
        Give the vengeance due
        To the valiant crew.
Behold how they toss their torches on high,
    How they point to the Persian abodes,
And glittering temples of their hostile gods !   145
The princes applaud with a furious joy ;
And the king seized a flambeau, with zeal to destroy ;
        Thais led the way,
        To light him to his prey,
And, like another Helen, fired another Troy.   150

CHORUS

And the king seized a flambeau, with zeal to destroy;
Thais led the way,
To light him to his prey,
And, like another Helen, fired another Troy.

VII

Thus long ago,   155
Ere heaving bellows learned to blow,
While organs yet were mute,
Timotheus, to his breathing flute
And sounding lyre,
Could swell the soul to rage, or kindle soft desire.   160
At last divine Cecilia came,
Inventress of the vocal frame ;
The sweet enthusiast, from her sacred store,
Enlarged the former narrow bounds,
And added length to solemn sounds,   165
With Nature's mother-wit, and arts unknown before.
Let old Timotheus yield the prize,
Or both divide the crown :
He raised a mortal to the skies ;
She drew an angel down.   170

GRAND CHORUS

At last divine Cecilia came,
Inventress of the vocal frame ;
The sweet enthusiast, from her sacred store,
Enlarged the former narrow bounds,
And added length to solemn sounds,   175
With Nature's mother-wit, and arts unknown before.
Let old Timotheus yield the prize,
Or both divide the crown :
He raised a mortal to the skies ;
She drew an angel down.   180

FABLES

Ancient and *Modern*;

Translated into VERSE,

FROM

Homer, Ovid, Boccace, & Chaucer:

WITH

ORIGINAL POEMS.

By Mr *DRYDEN.*

Nunc ultrò ad Cineres ipsius & ossa parentis
(Haud equidem sine mente, reor, sine numine divum)
Adsumus.   Virg. Æn. lib. 5.

LONDON:

Printed for *Jacob Tonson*, within *Gray's Inn Gate* next
Gray's Inn Lane.   MDCC.

CYMON and IPHIGENIA

FROM BOCCACE

'OLD as I am, for ladies' love unfit,
The power of beauty I remember yet,
Which once inflamed my soul, and still inspires my wit.

   .   .   .   .

In that sweet isle, where Venus keeps her court,   42
And every grace, and all the loves resort ;
Where either sex is formed of softer earth,
And takes the bent of pleasure from their birth ;   45
There lived a Cyprian lord, above the rest
Wise, wealthy, with a numerous issue blest.
  But as no gift of fortune is sincere,
Was only wanting in a worthy heir :
His eldest born, a goodly youth to view,   50
Excelled the rest in shape, and outward show ;
Fair, tall, his limbs with due proportion joined,
But of a heavy, dull, degenerate mind.
His soul belied the features of his face ;
Beauty was there, but beauty in disgrace.   55
A clownish mien, a voice with rustic sound,
And stupid eyes, that ever loved the ground.
He looked like Nature's error ; as the mind ⎫
And body were not of a piece designed, ⎬
But made for two, and by mistake in one were joined. ⎭ 60
  The ruling rod, the father's forming care,
Were exercised in vain on wit's despair ;
The more informed the less he understood,
And deeper sunk by floundering in the mud.
Now scorned of all, and grown the public shame,   65
The people from Galesus changed his name,

And Cymon called, which signifies a brute ;
So well his name did with his nature suit.

His father, when he found his labour lost,
And care employed that answered not the cost,   70
Chose an ungrateful object to remove,
And loathed to see what Nature made him love ;
So to his country farm the fool confined :
Rude work well suited with a rustic mind.
Thus to the wilds the sturdy Cymon went,   75
A squire among the swains, and pleased with banishment.
His corn and cattle were his only care,
And his supreme delight a country fair.

It happened on a summer's holiday,
That to the greenwood shade he took his way ;   80
For Cymon shunned the church, and used not much to pray.
His quarter-staff, which he could ne'er forsake,
Hung half before, and half behind his back.
He trudged along, unknowing what he sought,
And whistled as he went, for want of thought.   85

By chance conducted, or by thirst constrained,
The deep recesses of the grove he gained ;
Where in a plain, defended by the wood,
Crept through the matted grass a crystal flood,
By which an alabaster fountain stood :   90
And on the margin of the fount was laid
(Attended by her slaves) a sleeping maid ;
Like Dian and her nymphs, when, tired with sport,
To rest by cool Eurotas they resort :
The dame herself the goddess well expressed,   95
Not more distinguished by her purple vest,
Than by the charming features of her face,
And even in slumber a superior grace :
Her comely limbs composed with decent care,
Her body shaded with a slight cymar ;   100
Her bosom to the view was only bare :

Where two beginning paps were scarcely spied,
For yet their places were but signified :
The fanning wind upon her bosom blows,
To meet the fanning wind the bosom rose ;   105
The fanning wind and purling streams continue her repose.

  The fool of Nature stood with stupid eyes
And gaping mouth, that testified surprise,
Fixed on her face, nor could remove his sight,
New as he was to love, and novice in delight :   110
Long mute he stood, and leaning on his staff,
His wonder witnessed with an idiot laugh ;
Then would have spoke, but by his glimmering sense
First found his want of words, and feared offence :
Doubted for what he was he should be known,   115
By his clown accent, and his country tone.

  Through the rude chaos thus the running light
Shot the first ray that pierced the native night :
Then day and darkness in the mass were mixed,
Till gathered in a globe, the beams were fixed :   120
Last shone the sun, who radiant in his sphere
Illumined heaven and earth, and rolled around the year.
So reason in this brutal soul began :
Love made him first suspect he was a man ;
Love made him doubt his broad barbarian sound ;   125
By Love his want of words and wit he found :
That sense of want prepared the future way
To knowledge, and disclosed the promise of a day.

  What not his father's care, nor tutor's art
Could plant with pains in his unpolished heart,   130
The best instructor Love at once inspired,
As barren grounds to fruitfulness are fired ;
Love taught him shame, and shame with Love at strife
Soon taught the sweet civilities of life ;
His gross material soul at once could find   135
Somewhat in her excelling all her kind :

Exciting a desire till then unknown,
Somewhat unfound, or found in her alone.
This made the first impression in his mind,
Above, but just above, the brutal kind.   140
For beasts can like, but not distinguish too,
Nor their own liking by reflection know ;
Nor why they like or this or t'other face,
Or judge of this or that peculiar grace,
But love in gross, and stupidly admire ;   145
As flies allured by light, approach the fire.
Thus our man-beast advancing by degrees
First likes the whole, then separates what he sees ;
On several parts a several praise bestows,
The ruby lips, the well-proportioned nose,   150
The snowy skin, the raven-glossy hair,
The dimpled cheek, the forehead rising fair,
And even in sleep itself a smiling air.
From thence his eyes descending viewed the rest,
Her plump round arms, white hands, and heaving breast.
Long on the last he dwelt, though every part   156
A pointed arrow sped to pierce his heart.
   Thus in a trice a judge of beauty grown,
(A judge erected from a country clown)
He longed to see her eyes, in slumber hid,   160
And wished his own could pierce within the lid :
He would have waked her, but restrained his thought,
And love new-born the first good manners taught.
An awful fear his ardent wish withstood,
Nor durst disturb the goddess of the wood ;   165
For such she seemed by her celestial face,
Excelling all the rest of human race :
And things divine, by common sense he knew,
Must be devoutly seen at distant view :
So checking his desire, with trembling heart   170
Gazing he stood, nor would, nor could depart ;

Fixed as a pilgrim wildered in his way,
Who dares not stir by night for fear to stray ;
But stands with awful eyes to watch the dawn of day.

 At length awaking, Iphigene the fair   175
(So was the beauty called who caused his care)
Unclosed her eyes, and double day revealed,
While those of all her slaves in sleep were sealed.

 The slavering cudden, propped upon his staff,
Stood ready gaping with a grinning laugh,   180
To welcome her awake, nor durst begin
To speak, but wisely kept the fool within.
Then she : What make you Cymon here alone ?
(For Cymon's name was round the country known,
Because descended of a noble race,   185
And for a soul ill sorted with his face.)

 But still the sot stood silent with surprise,
With fixed regard on her new opened eyes,
And in his breast received the envenomed dart,
A tickling pain that pleased amid the smart.   190
But conscious of her form, with quick distrust
She saw his sparkling eyes, and feared his brutal lust :
This to prevent, she waked her sleepy crew,
And rising hasty took a short adieu.

 Then Cymon first his rustic voice essayed,   195
With proffered service to the parting maid
To see her safe ; his hand she long denied,
But took at length, ashamed of such a guide.
So Cymon led her home, and leaving there,
No more would to his country clowns repair,   200
But sought his father's house, with better mind,
Refusing in the farm to be confined.

 The father wondered at the son's return,
And knew not whether to rejoice or mourn ;
But doubtfully received, expecting still   205
To learn the secret causes of his altered will.

Nor was he long delayed ; the first request
He made, was like his brothers to be dressed,
And, as his birth required, above the rest.
  With ease his suit was granted by his sire,   210
Distinguishing his heir by rich attire :
His body thus adorned, he next designed
With liberal arts to cultivate his mind :
He sought a tutor of his own accord,
And studied lessons he before abhorred.   215
  Thus the man-child advanced, and learned so fast,
That in short time his equals he surpassed :
His brutal manners from his breast exiled,
His mien he fashioned, and his tongue he filed ;
In every exercise of all admired,   220
He seemed, nor only seemed, but was inspired :
Inspired by Love, whose business is to please ;
He rode, he fenced, he moved with graceful ease,
More famed for sense, for courtly carriage more,
Than for his brutal folly known before.   225
  What then of altered Cymon shall we say,
But that the fire which choked in ashes lay,
A load too heavy for his soul to move,
Was upward blown below, and brushed away by love ?
Love made an active progress through his mind,   230
The dusky parts he cleared, the gross refined ;
The drowsy waked ; and as he went impressed
The Maker's image on the human beast.
Thus was the man amended by desire,
And, though he loved perhaps with too much fire,   235
His father all his faults with reason scanned,
And liked an error of the better hand ;
Excused the excess of passion in his mind,
By flames too fierce, perhaps too much refined :
So Cymon, since his sire indulged his will,   240
Impetuous loved, and would be Cymon still ;

Galesus he disowned, and chose to bear
The name of Fool confirmed and bishoped by the fair.

  To Cipseus by his friends his suit he moved,
Cipseus the father of the fair he loved :   245
But he was pre-engaged by former ties,
While Cymon was endeavouring to be wise :
And Iphigene, obliged by former vows,
Had given her faith to wed a foreign spouse :
Her sire and she to Rhodian Pasimond,   250
Though both repenting, were by promise bound,
Nor could retract ; and thus, as Fate decreed,
Though better loved, he spoke too late to speed.

  The doom was past, the ship already sent
Did all his tardy diligence prevent :   255
Sighed to herself the fair unhappy maid,
While stormy Cymon thus in secret said :
The time is come for Iphigene to find
The miracle she wrought upon my mind ;
Her charms have made me man, her ravished love   260
In rank shall place me with the blessed above.
For mine by love, by force she shall be mine,
Or death, if force should fail, shall finish my design.

  Resolved he said : and rigged with speedy care
A vessel strong, and well equipped for war.   265
The secret ship with chosen friends he stored,
And bent to die, or conquer, went aboard.
Ambushed he lay behind the Cyprian shore,
Waiting the sail that all his wishes bore ;
Nor long expected, for the following tide   270
Sent out the hostile ship and beauteous bride.

  To Rhodes the rival bark directly steered,
When Cymon sudden at her back appeared,
And stopped her flight : then standing on his prow
In haughty terms he thus defied the foe :   275
Or strike your sails at summons, or prepare

To prove the last extremities of war.
Thus warned, the Rhodians for the fight provide ;
Already were the vessels side by side,
These obstinate to save, and those to seize the bride. 280
But Cymon soon his crooked grapples cast,
Which with tenacious hold his foes embraced,
And armed with sword and shield, amid the press he passed.
Fierce was the fight, but hastening to his prey,
By force the furious lover freed his way : 285
Himself alone dispersed the Rhodian crew,
The weak disdained, the valiant overthrew ;
Cheap conquest for his following friends remained,
He reaped the field, and they but only gleaned.

His victory confessed, the foes retreat, 290
And cast their weapons at the victor's feet.
Whom thus he cheered : O Rhodian youth, I fought
For love alone, nor other booty sought ;
Your lives are safe ; your vessel I resign,
Yours be your own, restoring what is mine : 295
In Iphigene I claim my rightful due,
Robbed by my rival, and detained by you :
Your Pasimond a lawless bargain drove,
The parent could not sell the daughter's love ;
Or if he could, my love disdains the laws, 300
And like a king by conquest gains his cause :
Where arms take place, all other pleas are vain ;
Love taught me force, and force shall love maintain.
You, what by strength you could not keep, release,
And at an easy ransom buy your peace. 305

Fear on the conquered side soon signed the accord,
And Iphigene to Cymon was restored.
While to his arms the blushing bride he took,
To seeming sadness she composed her look ;
As if by force subjected to his will, 310
Though pleased, dissembling, and a woman still.

And, for she wept, he wiped her falling tears,
And prayed her to dismiss her empty fears ;
For yours I am, he said, and have deserved
Your love much better, whom so long I served,   315
Than he to whom your formal father tied
Your vows ; and sold a slave, not sent a bride.
Thus while he spoke he seized the willing prey,
As Paris bore the Spartan spouse away :
Faintly she screamed, and even her eyes confessed   320
She rather would be thought, than was distressed.
 Who now exults but Cymon in his mind ?
Vain hopes and empty joys of human kind,
Proud of the present, to the future blind !
Secure of fate, while Cymon ploughs the sea,   325
And steers to Candy with his conquered prey.
Scarce the third glass of measured hours was run,
When like a fiery meteor sunk the sun ;
The promise of a storm ; the shifting gales
Forsake by fits and fill the flagging sails :   330
Hoarse murmurs of the main from far were heard,
And night came on, not by degrees prepared,
But all at once ; at once the winds arise,
The thunders roll, the forky lightning flies :
In vain the master issues out commands,   335
In vain the trembling sailors ply their hands :
The tempest unforeseen prevents their care,
And from the first they labour in despair.
The giddy ship, betwixt the winds and tides,
Forced back, and forwards, in a circle rides,   340
Stunned with the different blows ; then shoots amain
Till counterbuffed she stops, and sleeps again.
Not more aghast the proud archangel fell,
Plunged from the height of Heaven to deepest Hell,
Than stood the lover of his love possessed,   345
Now cursed the more, the more he had been blessed ;

More anxious for her danger than his own,
Death he defies ; but would be lost alone.
 Sad Iphigene to womanish complaints
Adds pious prayers, and wearies all the saints ;   350
Even if she could, her love she would repent,
But since she cannot, dreads the punishment :
Her forfeit faith and Pasimond betrayed
Are ever present, and her crime upbraid.
She blames herself, nor blames her lover less,   355
Augments her anger as her fears increase ;
From her own back the burden would remove,
And lays the load on his ungoverned love,
Which interposing durst in Heaven's despite
Invade, and violate another's right :   360
The powers incensed awhile deferred his pain,
And made him master of his vows in vain :
But soon they punished his presumptuous pride,
That for his daring enterprise she died,
Who rather not resisted, than complied.   365
 Then impotent of mind, with altered sense,
She hugged the offender, and forgave the offence,
Sex to the last : meantime with sails declined,
The wandering vessel drove before the wind :
Tossed, and retossed, aloft, and then alow ;   370
Nor port they seek, nor certain course they know,
But every moment wait the coming blow.
Thus blindly driven, by breaking day they viewed
The land before them, and their fears renewed ;
The land was welcome, but the tempest bore   375
The threatened ship against a rocky shore.
 A winding bay was near ; to this they bent,
And just escaped ; their force already spent.
Secure from storms, and panting from the sea,
The land unknown at leisure they survey ;   380
And saw (but soon their sickly sight withdrew)

The rising towers of Rhodes at distant view ;
And cursed the hostile shore of Pasimond,
Saved from the seas, and shipwrecked on the ground.
   The frighted sailors tried their strength in vain   385
To turn the stern, and tempt the stormy main ;
But the stiff wind withstood the labouring oar,
And forced them forward on the fatal shore !
The crooked keel now bites the Rhodian strand,
And the ship moored constrains the crew to land :   390
Yet still they might be safe, because unknown ;
But as ill fortune seldom comes alone,
The vessel they dismissed was driven before,
Already sheltered on their native shore ;
Known each, they know : but each with change of cheer ;
The vanquished side exults ; the victors fear ;   396
Not them but theirs, made prisoners ere they fight,
Despairing conquest, and deprived of flight.
   The country rings around with loud alarms,
And raw in fields the rude militia swarms ;   400
Mouths without hands ; maintained at vast expense,
In peace a charge, in war a weak defence :
Stout once a month they march, a blustering band,
And ever, but in times of need, at hand :
This was the morn when, issuing on the guard,   405
Drawn up in rank and file they stood prepared
Of seeming arms to make a short essay,
Then hasten to be drunk, the business of the day.
   The cowards would have fled, but that they knew
Themselves so many, and their foes so few ;   410
But crowding on, the last the first impel ;
Till overborne with weight the Cyprians fell.
Cymon enslaved, who first the war begun,
And Iphigene once more is lost and won.
   Deep in a dungeon was the captive cast,   415
Deprived of day, and held in fetters fast ;

His life was only spared at their request,
Whom taken he so nobly had released :
But Iphigenia was the ladies care,
Each in their turn addressed to treat the fair ;   420
While Pasimond and his the nuptial feast prepare.
  Her secret soul to Cymon was inclined,
But she must suffer what her fates assigned ;
So passive is the church of womankind.
What worse to Cymon could his fortune deal,   425
Rolled to the lowest spoke of all her wheel ?
It rested to dismiss the downward weight,
Or raise him upward to his former height ;
The latter pleased ; and love (concerned the most)
Prepared the amends, for what by love he lost.   430
  The sire of Pasimond had left a son,
Though younger, yet for courage early known,
Ormisda called ; to whom, by promise tied,
A Rhodian beauty was the destined bride :
Cassandra was her name, above the rest   435
Renowned for birth, with fortune amply blessed.
Lysymachus, who ruled the Rhodian state,
Was then by choice their annual magistrate :
He loved Cassandra too with equal fire,
But fortune had not favoured his desire ;   440
Crossed by her friends, by her not disapproved,
Nor yet preferred, or like Ormisda loved :
So stood the affair : some little hope remained,
That should his rival chance to lose, he gained.
  Meantime young Pasimond his marriage pressed,   445
Ordained the nuptial day, prepared the feast ;
And frugally resolved (the charge to shun,
Which would be double should he wed alone)
To join his brother's bridal with his own.
  Lysymachus oppressed with mortal grief   450
Received the news, and studied quick relief :

The fatal day approached : if force were used,
The magistrate his public trust abused ;
To justice liable, as law required ;
For when his office ceased, his power expired :   455
While power remained, the means were in his hand
By force to seize, and then forsake the land :
Betwixt extremes he knew not how to move,
A slave to fame, but more a slave to love :
Restraining others, yet himself not free,   460
Made impotent by power, debased by dignity !
Both sides he weighed : but after much debate,
The man prevailed above the magistrate.

    Love never fails to master what he finds,
But works a different way in different minds,   465
The fool enlightens, and the wise he blinds.
This youth proposing to possess, and scape,
Began in murder, to conclude in rape :
Unpraised by me, though Heaven sometime may bless
An impious act with undeserved success :   470
The great, it seems, are privileged alone
To punish all injustice but their own.
But here I stop, not daring to proceed,
Yet blush to flatter an unrighteous deed :
For crimes are but permitted, not decreed.   475

    Resolved on force, his wit the prætor bent
To find the means that might secure the event ;
Nor long he laboured, for his lucky thought
In captive Cymon found the friend he sought.
The example pleased : the cause and crime the same ; 480
An injured lover, and a ravished dame.
How much he durst he knew by what he dared ;
The less he had to lose, the less he cared
To menage loathsome life when love was the reward.

    This pondered well, and fixed on his intent,   485
In depth of night he for the prisoner sent ;

In secret sent, the public view to shun,
Then with a sober smile he thus begun :
The powers above, who bounteously bestow
Their gifts and graces on mankind below, 490
Yet prove our merit first, nor blindly give
To such as are not worthy to receive :
For valour and for virtue they provide
Their due reward, but first they must be tried :
These fruitful seeds within your mind they sowed ; 495
'Twas yours to improve the talent they bestowed :
They gave you to be born of noble kind,
They gave you love to lighten up your mind
And purge the grosser parts ; they gave you care
To please, and courage to deserve the fair. 500
  Thus far they tried you, and by proof they found
The grain entrusted in a grateful ground :
But still the great experiment remained,
They suffered you to lose the prize you gained ;
That you might learn the gift was theirs alone, 505
And, when restored, to them the blessing own.
Restored it soon will be ; the means prepared,
The difficulty smoothed, the danger shared :
Be but yourself, the care to me resign,
Then Iphigene is yours, Cassandra mine. 510
Your rival Pasimond pursues your life,
Impatient to revenge his ravished wife,
But yet not his ; to-morrow is behind,
And love our fortunes in one band has joined :
Two brothers are our foes ; Ormisda mine, 515
As much declared, as Pasimond is thine :
To-morrow must their common vows be tied ;
With love to friend, and fortune for our guide,
Let both resolve to die, or each redeem a bride.
  Right I have none, nor hast thou much to plead ; 520
'Tis force when done must justify the deed :

Our task performed, we next prepare for flight ;
And let the losers talk in vain of right :
We with the fair will sail before the wind ;
If they are grieved, I leave the laws behind.   525
Speak thy resolves ; if now thy courage droop,
Despair in prison, and abandon hope ;
But if thou darest in arms thy love regain,
(For liberty without thy love were vain :)
Then second my design to seize the prey,   530
Or lead to second rape, for well thou knowest the way.
   Said Cymon, overjoyed, Do thou propose
The means to fight, and only show the foes ;
For from the first, when love had fired my mind,
Resolved I left the care of life behind.   535
   To this the bold Lysymachus replied,
Let Heaven be neuter, and the sword decide :
The spousals are prepared, already play
The minstrels, and provoke the tardy day :
By this the brides are waked, their grooms are dressed ;
All Rhodes is summoned to the nuptial feast,   541
All but myself, the sole unbidden guest.
Unbidden though I am, I will be there,
And, joined by thee, intend to joy the fair.
   Now hear the rest ; when day resigns the light,   545
And cheerful torches guild the jolly night,
Be ready at my call ; my chosen few
With arms administered shall aid thy crew.
Then entering unexpected will we seize
Our destined prey, from men dissolved in ease,   550
By wine disabled, unprepared for fight ;
And hastening to the seas suborn our flight :
The seas are ours, for I command the fort,
A ship well manned expects us in the port :
If they, or if their friends, the prize contest,   555
Death shall attend the man who dares resist.

It pleased ! the prisoner to his hold retired,
His troop with equal emulation fired,
All fixed to fight, and all their wonted work required.
The sun arose ; the streets were thronged around, 560
The palace opened, and the posts were crowned :
The double bridegroom at the door attends
The expected spouse, and entertains the friends :
They meet, they lead to church ; the priests invoke
The powers, and feed the flames with fragrant smoke : 565
This done they feast, and at the close of night
By kindled torches vary their delight,
These lead the lively dance, and those the brimming bowls
        invite.
Now, at the appointed place and hour assigned,
With souls resolved the ravishers were joined :   570
Three bands are formed : the first is sent before
To favour the retreat and guard the shore :
The second at the palace gate is placed,
And up the lofty stairs ascend the last :
A peaceful troop they seem with shining vests,   575
But coats of mail beneath secure their breasts.
Dauntless they enter, Cymon at their head,
And find the feast renewed, the table spread :
Sweet voices mixed with instrumental sounds
Ascend the vaulted roof, the vaulted roof rebounds. 580
When like the harpies rushing through the hall
The sudden troop appears, the tables fall,
Their smoking load is on the pavement thrown ;
Each ravisher prepares to seize his own :
The brides invaded with a rude embrace   585
Shriek out for aid, confusion fills the place :
Quick to redeem the prey their plighted lords
Advance, the palace gleams with shining swords.
But late is all defence, and succour vain ;
The rape is made, the ravishers remain :   590

Two sturdy slaves were only sent before
To bear the purchased prize in safety to the shore.
The troop retires, the lovers close the rear,
With forward faces not confessing fear :
Backward they move, but scorn their pace to mend,
Then seek the stairs, and with slow haste descend.   596
   Fierce Pasimond, their passage to prevent,
Thrust full on Cymon's back in his descent,
The blade returned unbathed, and to the handle bent :
Stout Cymon soon remounts, and cleft in two   600
His rival's head with one descending blow :
And as the next in rank Ormisda stood,
He turned the point ; the sword inured to blood
Bored his unguarded breast, which poured a purple flood.
   With vowed revenge the gathering crowd pursues, 605
The ravishers turn head, the fight renews ;
The hall is heaped with corps ; the sprinkled gore
Besmears the walls, and floats the marble floor.
Dispersed at length the drunken squadron flies,
The victors to their vessel bear the prize,   610
And hear behind loud groans, and lamentable cries.
   The crew with merry shouts their anchors weigh,
Then ply their oars, and brush the buxom sea,
While troops of gathered Rhodians crowd the quay.
What should the people do, when left alone ?   615
The governor and government are gone ;
The public wealth to foreign parts conveyed ;
Some troops disbanded, and the rest unpaid.
Rhodes is the sovereign of the sea no more ;
Their ships unrigged, and spent their naval store ;   620
They neither could defend, nor can pursue,
But grind their teeth, and cast a helpless view :
In vain with darts a distant war they try,
Short, and more short, the missive weapons fly.
Meanwhile the ravishers their crimes enjoy,   625

And flying sails and sweeping oars employ :
The cliffs of Rhodes in little space are lost ;
Jove's Isle they seek ; nor Jove denies his coast.
  In safety landed on the Candian shore,
With generous wines their spirits they restore ;   630
There Cymon with his Rhodian friend resides,
Both court and wed at once the willing brides.
A war ensues, the Cretans own their cause,
Stiff to defend their hospitable laws :
Both parties lose by turns ; and neither wins,   635
Till peace propounded by a truce begins.
The kindred of the slain forgive the deed,
But a short exile must for show precede ;
The term expired, from Candia they remove ;
And happy each at home enjoys his love.   640

SONGS and LYRICAL PASSAGES

Ah fading joy, how quickly art thou past !
  Yet we thy ruin haste :
As if the cares of human life were few,
  We seek out new,
And follow Fate that does too fast pursue.   5

See how on every bough the birds express
  In their sweet notes their happiness.
  They all enjoy and nothing spare ;
But on their Mother Nature lay their care :
Why then should man, the lord of all below   10
  Such troubles choose to know,
As none of all his subjects undergo ?
The Indian Emperor, 1667, Act IV, Scene **iii.**

I feed a flame within which so torments me
That it both pains my heart, and yet contents me :
'Tis such a pleasing smart and I so love it,
That I had rather die, than once remove it.

Yet he for whom I grieve shall never know it,   5
My tongue does not betray, nor my eyes show it :
Not a sigh, not a tear my pain discloses,
But they fall silently like dew on roses.

Thus to prevent my love from being cruel,
My heart 's the sacrifice as 'tis the fuel :   10
And while I suffer thus to give him quiet,
My faith rewards my love, though he deny it.

The Maiden Queen, 1668, Act IV, Scene ii.

Ah how sweet it is to love,
Ah how gay is young desire !
And what pleasing pains we prove
When we first approach love's fire !
  Pains of love be sweeter far   5
  Than all other pleasures are.

Love and time with reverence use,
Treat 'em like a parting friend :
Nor the golden gifts refuse
Which in youth sincere they send :   10
  For each year their price is more,
  And they less simple than before.

Tyrannic Love, 1670, Act IV, Scene i.

After the pangs of a desperate lover,
  When day and night I have sighed all in vain,
Ah what a pleasure it is to discover
  In her eyes pity, who causes my pain !

When with unkindness our love at a stand is, 5
  And both have punished ourselves with the pain,
Ah what a pleasure the touch of her hand is,
  Ah what a pleasure to press it again !

An Evening's Love, 1671, Act II, Scene i.

Wherever I am, and whatever I do,
  My Phyllis is still in my mind :
When angry I mean not to Phyllis to go,
  My feet of themselves the way find :
Unknown to myself I am just at her door, 5
And when I would rail, I can bring out no more
  Than Phyllis too fair and unkind !

Alas, I discover too much of my love,
  And she too well knows her own power !
She makes me each day a new martyrdom prove, 10
  And makes me grow jealous each hour :
But let her each minute torment my poor mind,
I had rather love Phyllis both false and unkind,
  Than ever be freed from her power.

The Conquest of Granada, Part I, 1672, Act IV, Scene ii.

Farewell ungrateful traitor,
  Farewell my perjured swain,
Let never injured creature
  Believe a man again.
The pleasure of possessing 5
Surpasses all expressing,
But 'tis too short a blessing,
  And love too long a pain.

The Spanish Friar, 1681, Act V, Scene i.

(The River Thames Speaks)

Old father Ocean calls my tide ;
Come away, come away ;
The barks upon the billows ride,
The master will not stay ;
The merry boatswain from his side   5
His whistle takes to check and chide
The lingering lads' delay,
And all the crew aloud has cried,
Come away, come away.

Albion and Albanius, 1685, Act II.

(Song of the Nereids)

From the low palace of old father Ocean
Come we in pity your cares to deplore ;
Sea-racing dolphins are trained for our motion,
Moony tides swelling to roll us ashore.

Albion and Albanius, 1685, Act III.

Song of Venus

FAIREST Isle, all isles excelling,
    Seat of pleasures, and of loves ;
Venus here will choose her dwelling,
    And forsake her Cyprian groves.

Cupid from her favourite nation   5
    Care and envy will remove ;
Jealousy that poisons passion,
    And despair that dies for love.

Every swain shall pay his duty,
    Grateful every nymph shall prove ;   10
And as these excel in beauty,
    Those shall be renown'd for love.

King Arthur, 1691, Act V.

No, no, poor suffering heart, no change endeavour,
Choose to sustain the smart, rather than leave her ;
My ravished eyes behold such charms about her,
I can die with her, but not live without her.
One tender sigh of hers to see me languish,   5
Will more than pay the price of my past anguish :
Beware, O cruel fair, how you smile on me,
'Twas a kind look of yours that has undone me.

Cleomenes, 1692, Act II, **Scene ii.**

A Song to a fair young Lady going out of Town in the Spring

Ask not the cause why sullen Spring
   So long delays her flowers to bear ;
Why warbling birds forget to sing,
   And winter storms invert the year ?
Chloris is gone ; and Fate provides   5
To make it Spring, where she resides.

Chloris is gone, the cruel fair ;
   She cast not back a pitying eye :
But left her lover in despair,
   To sigh, to languish, and to die :   10
Ah, how can those fair eyes endure
To give the wounds they will not cure !

Great God of Love, why hast thou made
   A face that can all hearts command,
That all religions can invade,   15
   And change the laws of every land ?
Where thou hadst placed such power before,
Thou shouldst have made her mercy more.

When Chloris to the temple comes,
    Adoring crowds before her fall ;   20
She can restore the dead from tombs,
    And every life but mine recall.
I only am by love designed
To be the victim for mankind.

Printed in Miscellany Poems, 1693.

(*The Seventeenth Century*)

Momus. All, all of a piece throughout :
   Pointing to Diana. Thy chase had a beast in view ;
     to Mars.   Thy wars brought nothing about ;
     to Venus.   Thy lovers were all untrue.
Janus. 'Tis well an old age is out.   5
Chronos. And time to begin a new.

Chorus of all. *All, all of a piece throughout :*
    Thy chase had a beast in view ;
    Thy wars brought nothing about ;
    Thy lovers were all untrue.   10
    'Tis well an old age is out,
    And time to begin a new.

The Secular Masque, 1700.

Of Dramatic Poesy

AN ESSAY

1668; revised 1684

The Introduction

It was that memorable day, in the first summer of the late war, when our navy engaged the Dutch ; a day wherein the two most mighty and best appointed fleets which any age had ever seen, disputed the command of the greater half of the globe, the commerce of nations, and the riches of the universe. While these vast floating bodies, on either side, moved against each other in parallel lines, and our countrymen, under the happy conduct of his Royal Highness, went breaking, by little and little, into the line of the enemies ; the noise of the cannon from both navies reached our ears about the City, so that all men being alarmed with it, and in a dreadful suspense of the event which they knew was then deciding, every one went following the sound as his fancy led him ; and leaving the town almost empty, some took towards the park, some cross the river, others down it ; all seeking the noise in the depth of silence.

Among the rest, it was the fortune of Eugenius, Crites, Lisideius, and Neander, to be in company together ; three of them persons whom their wit and quality have made known to all the town ; and whom I have chose to hide under these borrowed names, that they may not suffer by so ill a relation as I am going to make of their discourse.

Taking then a barge which a servant of Lisideius had provided for them, they made haste to shoot the bridge, and left behind them that great fall of waters which

hindered them from hearing what they desired : after
which, having disengaged themselves from many vessels
which rode at anchor in the Thames, and almost blocked
up the passage towards Greenwich, they ordered the
watermen to let fall their oars more gently ; and then,
every one favouring his own curiosity with a strict silence,
it was not long ere they perceived the air to break about
them like the noise of distant thunder, or of swallows in
a chimney : those little undulations of sound, though
10 almost vanishing before they reached them, yet still
seeming to retain somewhat of their first horror, which
they had betwixt the fleets. After they had attentively
listened till such time as the sound by little and little
went from them, Eugenius, lifting up his head, and taking
notice of it, was the first who congratulated to the rest that
happy omen of our Nation's victory : adding, that we had
but this to desire in confirmation of it, that we might hear
no more of that noise, which was now leaving the English
coast. When the rest had concurred in the same opinion,
20 Crites, a person of a sharp judgement, and somewhat too
delicate a taste in wit, which the world have mistaken
in him for ill-nature, said, smiling to us, that if the concernment of this battle had not been so exceeding great,
he could scarce have wished the victory at the price he
knew he must pay for it, in being subject to the reading
and hearing of so many ill verses as he was sure would be
made on that subject : adding, that no argument could
scape some of those eternal rhymers, who watch a battle with
more diligence than the ravens and birds of prey, and the
30 worst of them surest to be first in upon the quarry ; while
the better able either out of modesty writ not at all, or
set that due value upon their poems, as to let them be often
desired and long expected. 'There are some of those im-
pertinent people of whom you speak,' answered Lisideius,
'who to my knowledge are already so provided, either

way, that they can produce not only a Panegyric upon the
victory, but, if need be, a Funeral Elegy on the Duke; wherein, after they have crowned his valour with many laurels,
they will at last deplore the odds under which he fell, concluding that his courage deserved a better destiny.' All
the company smiled at the conceit of Lisideius; but Crites,
more eager than before, began to make particular exceptions against some writers, and said, the public magistrate
ought to send betimes to forbid them; and that it concerned the peace and quiet of all honest people, that ill 10
poets should be as well silenced as seditious preachers.
'In my opinion,' replied Eugenius, 'you pursue your
point too far; for as to my own particular, I am so great
a lover of poesy, that I could wish them all rewarded,
who attempt but to do well; at least, I would not have
them worse used than one of their brethren was by
Sylla the Dictator: *Quem in concione vidimus* (says
Tully) *cum ei libellum malus poeta de populo subjecisset,
quod epigramma in eum fecisset tantummodo alternis versibus
longiusculis, statim ex iis rebus quas tunc vendebat jubere* 20
ei praemium tribui, sub ea conditione ne quid postea scriberet.
'I could wish with all my heart,' replied Crites, 'that
many whom we know were as bountifully thanked upon
the same condition,—that they would never trouble us
again. For amongst others, I have a mortal apprehension
of two poets, whom this victory, with the help of both her
wings, will never be able to escape.' ' 'Tis easy to guess
whom you intend,' said Lisideius; ' and without naming
them, I ask you, if one of them does not perpetually pay
us with clenches upon words, and a certain clownish kind 30
of raillery? if now and then he does not offer at a catachresis or Clevelandism, wresting and torturing a word
into another meaning: in fine, if he be not one of those
whom the French would call *un mauvais buffon*; one who is
so much a well-willer to the satire, that he intends at least

to spare no man ; and though he cannot strike a blow to hurt any, yet he ought to be punished for the malice of the action, as our witches are justly hanged, because they think themselves to be such, and suffer deservedly for believing they did mischief, because they meant it.'   ' You have described him,' said Crites, 'so exactly, that I am afraid to come after you with my other extremity of poetry.   He is one of those who, having had some advantage of education and converse, knows better than the other what a poet should be, but puts it into practice more unluckily than any man ; his style and matter are everywhere alike : he is the most calm, peaceable writer you ever read : he never disquiets your passions with the least concernment, but still leaves you in as even a temper as he found you ; he is a very Leveller in poetry : he creeps along with ten little words in every line, and helps out his numbers with *For to*, and *Unto*, and all the pretty expletives he can find, till he drags them to the end of another line ; while the sense is left tired half way behind it : he doubly starves all his verses, first for want of thought, and then of expression ; his poetry neither has wit in it, nor seems to have it ; like him in Martial :

Pauper videri Cinna *vult, et est pauper.*

' He affects plainness, to cover his want of imagination : when he writes the serious way, the highest flight of his fancy is some miserable antithesis, or seeming contradiction ; and in the comic he is still reaching at some thin conceit, the ghost of a jest, and that too flies before him, never to be caught ; these swallows which we see before us on the Thames are the just resemblance of his wit : you may observe how near the water they stoop, how many proffers they make to dip, and yet how seldom they touch it ; and when they do, 'tis but the surface : they skim over it but to catch a gnat, and then mount into the air and leave it.'

'Well, gentlemen,' said Eugenius, 'you may speak your pleasure of these authors; but though I and some few more about the town may give you a peaceable hearing, yet assure yourselves, there are multitudes who would think you malicious and them injured: especially him whom you first described; he is the very Withers of the city: they have bought more editions of his works than would serve to lay under all their pies at the Lord Mayor's Christmas. When his famous poem first came out in the year 1660, I have seen them reading it in the midst of 'Change time; nay, so vehement they were at it, that they lost their bargain by the candles' ends. But what will you say if he has been received amongst great persons? I can assure you he is, this day, the envy of one who is lord in the art of quibbling; and who does not take it well, that any man should intrude so far into his province.' 'All I would wish,' replied Crites, 'is that they who love his writings, may still admire him, and his fellow poet: *Qui Bavium non odit, &c.*, is curse sufficient.' 'And farther,' added Lisideius, 'I believe there is no man who writes well but would think he had hard measure if their admirers should praise anything of his: *Nam quos contemnimus, eorum quoque laudes contemnimus.*' 'There are so few who write well in this age,' says Crites, 'that methinks any praises should be welcome; they neither rise to the dignity of the last age, nor to any of the Ancients: and we may cry out of the writers of this time, with more reason than Petronius, of his *Pace vestrâ liceat dixisse, primi omnium eloquentiam perdidistis*: you have debauched the true old poetry so far, that Nature, which is the soul of it, is not in any of your writings.'

'If your quarrel,' said Eugenius, 'to those who now write, be grounded only on your reverence to antiquity, there is no man more ready to adore those great Greeks and Romans than I am: but on the other side, I cannot

think so contemptibly of the age in which I live, or so dis-
honourably of my own country, as not to judge we equal
the Ancients in most kinds of poesy, and in some surpass
them ; neither know I any reason why I may not be as
zealous for the reputation of our age, as we find the Ancients
themselves were in reference to those who lived before
them.   For you hear your Horace saying,

> *Indignor quidquam reprehendi, non quia crasse*
> *Compositum, illepidève putetur, sed quia nuper.*

10 And after :

> *Si meliora dies, ut vina, poemata reddit,*
> *Scire velim, pretium chartis quotus arroget annus ?*

'But I see I am engaging in a wide dispute, where the
arguments are not like to reach close on either side ; for
Poesy is of so large an extent, and so many both of the
Ancients and Moderns have done well in all kinds of it,
that in citing one against the other, we shall take up more
time this evening than each man's occasions will allow
him : therefore I would ask Crites to what part of Poesy
20 he would confine his arguments, and whether he would
defend the general cause of the Ancients against the
Moderns, or oppose any age of the Moderns against this
of ours ? '

Crites, a little while considering upon this demand, told
Eugenius that if he pleased, he would limit their dispute
to Dramatic Poesy ; in which he thought it not difficult to
prove, either that the Ancients were superior to the Moderns,
or the last age to this of ours.

Eugenius was somewhat surprised, when he heard
30 Crites make choice of that subject. 'For ought I see,'
said he, 'I have undertaken a harder province than
I imagined ; for though I never judged the plays of the
Greek or Roman poets comparable to ours, yet, on the
other side, those we now see acted come short of many
which were written in the last age : but my comfort is,

if we are o'ercome, it will be only by our own countrymen : and if we yield to them in this one part of poesy, we more surpass them in all the other : for in the epic or lyric way, it will be hard for them to show us one such amongst them, as we have many now living, or who lately were : they can produce nothing so courtly writ, or which expresses so much the conversation of a gentleman, as Sir John Suckling ; nothing so even, sweet, and flowing, as Mr. Waller ; nothing so majestic, so correct, as Sir John Denham ; nothing so elevated, so copious, and full of spirit, as Mr. Cowley ; as for the Italian, French, and Spanish plays, I can make it evident, that those who now write surpass them ; and that the Drama is wholly ours.'

All of them were thus far of Eugenius his opinion, that the sweetness of English verse was never understood or practised by our fathers ; even Crites himself did not much oppose it : and every one was willing to acknowledge how much our poesy is improved by the happiness of some writers yet living ; who first taught us to mould our thoughts into easy and significant words ; to retrench the superfluities of expression, and to make our rhyme so properly a part of the verse, that it should never mislead the sense, but itself be led and governed by it.

Shakespeare, Beaumont and Fletcher, and Ben Jonson

As Neander was beginning to examine *The Silent Woman*, Eugenius, earnestly regarding him, ' I beseech you, Neander,' said he, ' gratify the company, and me in particular, so far as, before you speak of the play, to give us a character of the author ; and tell us frankly your opinion, whether you do not think all writers, both French and English, ought to give place to him.'

'I fear,' replied Neander, 'that in obeying your commands I shall draw some envy on myself. Besides, in performing them, it will be first necessary to speak somewhat of Shakespeare and Fletcher, his rivals in poesy ; and one of them, in my opinion, at least his equal, perhaps his superior.

'To begin, then, with Shakespeare. He was the man who of all modern, and perhaps ancient poets, had the largest and most comprehensive soul. All the images of
10 Nature were still present to him, and he drew them, not laboriously, but luckily ; when he describes anything, you more than see it, you feel it too. Those who accuse him to have wanted learning, give him the greater commendation : he was naturally learned ; he needed not the spectacles of books to read Nature ; he looked inwards, and found her there. I cannot say he is everywhere alike ; were he so, I should do him injury to compare him with the greatest of mankind. He is many times flat, insipid ; his comic wit degenerating into clenches, his serious swelling
20 into bombast. But he is always great, when some great occasion is presented to him ; no man can say he ever had a fit subject for his wit, and did not then raise himself as high above the rest of poets,

Quantum lenta solent inter viburna cupressi.

The consideration of this made Mr. Hales of Eaton say, that there was no subject of which any poet ever writ, but he would produce it much better done in Shakespeare ; and however others are now generally preferred before him, yet the age wherein he lived, which had con-
30 temporaries with him Fletcher and Jonson, never equalled them to him in their esteem : and in the last King's court, when Ben's reputation was at highest, Sir John Suckling, and with him the greater part of the courtiers, set our Shakespeare far above him.

'Beaumont and Fletcher, of whom I am next to speak,

had, with the advantage of Shakespeare's wit, which was their precedent, great natural gifts, improved by study : Beaumont espècially being so accurate a judge of plays, that Ben Jonson, while he lived, submitted all his writings to his censure, and, 'tis thought, used his judgment in correcting, if not contriving, all his plots. What value he had for him, appears by the verses he writ to him ; and therefore I need speak no farther of it. The first play that brought Fletcher and him in esteem was their *Philaster* : for before that, they had written two or three 10 very unsuccessfully, as the like is reported of Ben Jonson, before he writ *Every Man in his Humour*. Their plots were generally more regular than Shakespeare's, especially those which were made before Beaumont's death ; and they understood and imitated the conversation of gentlemen much better ; whose wild debaucheries, and quickness of wit in repartees, no poet before them could paint as they have done. Humour, which Ben Jonson derived from particular persons, they made it not their business to describe : they represented all the passions very lively, but above all, 20 love. I am apt to believe the English language in them arrived to its highest perfection : what words have since been taken in, are rather superfluous than ornamental. Their plays are now the most pleasant and frequent entertainments of the stage ; two of theirs being acted through the year for one of Shakespeare's or Jonson's : the reason is, because there is a certain gaiety in their comedies, and pathos in their more serious plays, which suits generally with all men's humours. Shakespeare's language is likewise a little obsolete, and Ben Jonson's wit comes short 30 of theirs.

' As for Jonson, to whose character I am now arrived, if we look upon him while he was himself (for his last plays were but his dotages), I think him the most learned and judicious writer which any theatre ever had. He was a most severe judge of himself, as well as others.

One cannot say he wanted wit, but rather that he was frugal of it. In his works you find little to retrench or alter. Wit, and language, and humour also in some measure, we had before him ; but something of art was wanting to the Drama, till he came. He managed his strength to more advantage than any who preceded him. You seldom find him making love in any of his scenes, or endeavouring to move the passions ; his genius was too sullen and saturnine to do it gracefully, especially when he knew he came after those who had performed both to such an height. Humour was his proper sphere ; and in that he delighted most to represent mechanic people. He was deeply conversant in the Ancients, both Greek and Latin, and he borrowed boldly from them : there is scarce a poet or historian among the Roman authors of those times whom he has not translated in *Sejanus* and *Catiline*. But he has done his robberies so openly, that one may see he fears not to be taxed by any law. He invades authors like a monarch ; and what would be theft in other poets, is only victory in him. With the spoils of these writers he so represents old Rome to us, in its rites, ceremonies, and customs, that if one of their poets had written either of his tragedies, we had seen less of it than in him. If there was any fault in his language, 'twas that he weaved it too closely and laboriously, in his comedies especially : perhaps too, he did a little too much Romanize our tongue, leaving the words which he translated almost as much Latin as he found them : wherein, though he learnedly followed their language, he did not enough comply with the idiom of ours. If I would compare him with Shakespeare, I must acknowledge him the more correct poet, but Shakespeare the greater wit. Shakespeare was the Homer, or father of our dramatic poets ; Jonson was the Virgil, the pattern of elaborate writing ; I admire him, but I love Shakespeare.'

A Discourse concerning the Original
and Progress of S A T I R E

Dated ' Aug. 18. 1692 '

Prefixed to the translation of Juvenal, 1693

Dryden's Epic

THUS, my Lord, I have, as briefly as I could, given your Lordship, and by you the world, a rude draught of what I have been long labouring in my imagination, and what I had intended to have put in practice, (though far unable for the attempt of such a poem,) and to have left the stage, (to which my genius never much inclined me,) for a work which would have taken up my life in the performance of it. This, too, I had intended chiefly for the honour of my native country, to which a poet is particularly obliged. Of two subjects, both relating to 10 it, I was doubtful whether I should choose that of King Arthur conquering the Saxons, which, being farther distant in time, gives the greater scope to my invention ; or that of Edward, the Black Prince, in subduing Spain, and restoring it to the lawful prince, though a great tyrant, Don Pedro the Cruel : which for the compass of time, including only the expedition of one year ; for the greatness of the action, and its answerable event ; for the magnanimity of the English hero, opposed to the ingratitude of the person whom he restored ; and for 20 the many beautiful episodes, which I had interwoven with the principal design, together with the characters of the chiefest English persons ; wherein, after Virgil and Spenser, I would have taken occasion to represent my living friends and patrons of the noblest families, and also shadowed the events of future ages, in the succession of our imperial line ; with these helps, and those of the machines, which I have mentioned, I might perhaps have done as well as some of my predecessors, or at least chalked out a way for others to amend my errors in a like design. But being encouraged only with fair words by King Charles II, my little salary ill paid, and no prospect of a future subsistence, I was then discouraged in the beginning of my attempt ; and now age has overtaken me, and want, a more insufferable evil, through the change of the times, has wholly disenabled me. Though I must ever acknowledge, to the honour of your Lordship, and the eternal memory of your charity, that, since this Revolution, wherein I have patiently suffered the ruin of my small fortune, and the loss of that poor subsistence which I had from two kings, whom I had served more faithfully than profitably to myself ; then your Lordship was pleased, out of no other motive but your own nobleness, without any desert of mine, or the least solicitation from me, to make me a most bountiful present, which at that time, when I was most in want of it, came most seasonably and unexpectedly to my relief. That favour, my Lord, is of itself sufficient to bind any grateful man to a perpetual acknowledgment, and to all the future service which one of my mean condition can ever be able to perform. May the Almighty God return it for me, both in blessing you here, and rewarding you hereafter ! I must not presume to defend the cause for which I now suffer, because your Lordship is engaged against it ; but the more you are so, the greater is my obligation to you, for your laying aside all the considerations of factions and parties, to do an action of pure disinteressed charity.

Personal Satire

That former sort of satire, which is known in England by the name of lampoon, is a dangerous sort of weapon, and for the most part unlawful. We have no moral right on the reputation of other men. 'Tis taking from them what we cannot restore to them. There are only two reasons for which we may be permitted to write lampoons ; and I will not promise that they can always justify us. The first is revenge, when we have been affronted in the same nature, or have been any ways notoriously abused, and can make ourselves no other reparation. And yet we know, that, in Christian charity, all offences are to be forgiven, as we expect the like pardon for those which we daily commit against Almighty God. And this considera-tion has often made me tremble when I was saying our Saviour's prayer ; for the plain condition of the forgive-ness which we beg is the pardoning of others the offences which they have done to us ; for which reason I have many times avoided the commission of that fault, even when I have been notoriously provoked. Let not this, my Lord, pass for vanity in me ; for it is truth. More libels have been written against me, than almost any man now living ; and I had reason on my side, to have defended my own innocence. I speak not of my poetry, which I have wholly given up to the critics : let them use it as they please : posterity, perhaps, may be more favourable to me ; for interest and passion will lie buried in another age, and partiality and prejudice be forgotten. I speak of my morals, which have been sufficiently aspersed : that only sort of reputation ought to be dear to every honest man, and is to me. But let the world witness for me, that I have been often wanting to myself in that particular ; I have seldom answered any scurrilous lam-poon, when it was in my power to have exposed my

enemies : and, being naturally vindicative, have suffered
in silence, and possessed my soul in quiet.

Anything, though never so little, which a man speaks
of himself, in my opinion, is still too much ; and therefore I will waive this subject, and proceed to give the
second reason which may justify a poet when he writes
against a particular person ; and that is, when he is
become a public nuisance. All those, whom Horace in
his Satires, and Persius and Juvenal have mentioned in
10 theirs, with a brand of infamy, are wholly such. 'Tis an
action of virtue to make examples of vicious men. They
may and ought to be upbraided with their crimes and
follies ; both for their own amendment, if they are not
yet incorrigible, and for the terror of others, to hinder
them from falling into those enormities which they see
are so severely punished in the persons of others. The
first reason was only an excuse for revenge ; but this
second is absolutely of a poet's office to perform : but
how few lampooners are there now living, who are capable
20 of this duty ! When they come in my way, 'tis impossible
sometimes to avoid reading them. But, good God, how
remote they are, in common justice, from the choice of
such persons as are the proper subject of satire ! And
how little wit they bring for the support of their injustice !
The weaker sex is their most ordinary theme ; and the
best and fairest are sure to be the most severely handled.
Amongst men, those who are prosperously unjust are
entitled to a panegyric ; but afflicted virtue is insolently
stabbed with all manner of reproaches. No decency is
30 considered, no fulsomeness omitted ; no venom is wanting,
as far as dulness can supply it. For there is a perpetual
dearth of wit ; a barrenness of good sense and entertainment. The neglect of the readers will soon put an end to
this sort of scribbling. There can be no pleasantry where
there is no wit ; no impression can be made where there

is no truth for the foundation. To conclude, they are like the fruits of the earth in this unnatural season : the corn which held up its head is spoiled with rankness ; but the greater part of the harvest is laid along, and little of good income and wholesome nourishment is received into the barns.

Fine Raillery

Thus I have treated in a new method the comparison betwixt Horace, Juvenal, and Persius ; somewhat of their particular manner belonging to all of them is yet remaining to be considered. Persius was grave, and particularly opposed his gravity to lewdness, which was the predominant vice in Nero's court, at the time when he published his Satires, which was before that emperor fell into the excess of cruelty. Horace was a mild admonisher, a court satirist, fit for the gentle times of Augustus, and more fit, for the reasons which I have already given. Juvenal was as proper for his times, as they for theirs ; his was an age that deserved a more severe chastisement ; vices were more gross and open, more flagitious, more encouraged by the example of a tyrant, and more protected by his authority. Therefore, wheresoever Juvenal mentions Nero, he means Domitian, whom he dares not attack in his own person, but scourges him by proxy. Heinsius urges in praise of Horace, that, according to the ancient art and law of satire, it should be nearer to comedy than tragedy ; not declaiming against vice, but only laughing at it. Neither Persius nor Juvenal were ignorant of this, for they had both studied Horace. And the thing itself is plainly true. But as they had read Horace, they had likewise read Lucilius, of whom Persius says *secuit urbem ; . . . et genuinum fregit in illis* ; meaning Mutius and Lupus ; and Juvenal also mentions him in these words : *Ense velut stricto, quoties Lucilius ardens infremuit*, &c. So that they thought the imitation of Lucilius was more proper to their purpose than that of Horace. They changed satire, says Holyday ; but they changed it for the better : for the business being to reform great vices, chastisement goes further than admonition ; whereas a perpetual grin, like that of Horace, does rather anger than amend a man.

Thus far that learned critic, Barten Holyday, whose interpretation and illustrations of Juvenal are as excellent as the verse of his translation and his English are lame and pitiful. For 'tis not enough to give us the meaning of a poet, which I acknowledge him to have performed most faithfully, but he must also imitate his genius and his numbers, as far as the English will come up to the elegance of the original. In few words, 'tis only for a poet to translate a poem. Holyday and Stapylton had not enough considered this, when they attempted Juvenal : but I forbear reflections ; only I beg leave to take notice of this sentence, where Holyday says, *a perpetual grin, like that of Horace, rather angers than amends a man.* I cannot give him up the manner of Horace in low satire so easily. Let the chastisement of Juvenal be never so necessary for his new kind of satire ; let him declaim as wittily and sharply as he pleases ; yet still the nicest and most delicate touches of satire consist in fine raillery. This, my Lord, is your particular talent, to which even Juvenal could not arrive. 'Tis not reading, 'tis not imitation of an author, which can produce this fineness ; it must be inborn ; it must proceed from a genius, and particular way of thinking, which is not to be taught ; and therefore not to be imitated by him who has it not from nature. How easy is it to call rogue and villain, and that wittily ! But how hard to make a man appear a fool, a blockhead, or a knave, without using any of those opprobrious terms ! To spare the grossness of the names, and to do the thing yet more severely, is to draw a full face, and to make the nose and cheeks stand out, and yet not to employ any depth of shadowing. This is the mystery of that noble trade, which yet no master can teach to his apprentice ; he may give the rules, but the scholar is never the nearer in his practice. Neither is it true that this fineness of raillery is offensive. A witty man is tickled while he is hurt in this manner, and a fool feels it not. The occasion of an offence may possibly be given, but he cannot take it. If it be granted that in effect this way does more mischief ; that a man is secretly wounded, and though he be not sensible himself, yet the malicious world will find it out for him ; yet there is still a vast difference betwixt the slovenly butchering of a man, and the fineness of a stroke that separates the head from the body, and leaves it standing in its place. A man may be capable, as Jack Ketch's wife said of his servant, of a plain piece of work, a bare hanging ; but to make a malefactor die sweetly was only belonging to her husband. I wish I could apply it to myself, if the reader would be kind enough to think it belongs to me. The character of Zimri in my *Absalom* is, in my opinion, worth the whole poem : it is not bloody, but it is ridiculous enough ; and he for whom it was intended, was too witty to resent it as an injury. If I had railed, I might have suffered for it justly ; but I managed my own work more happily, perhaps more dexterously. I avoided the mention of great crimes, and applied myself to the representing of blindsides, and little extravagancies ; to which, the wittier a man is, he is generally the more obnoxious. It succeeded as I wished ; the jest went round, and he was laughed at in his turn who began the frolic.

The Preface to

FABLES

Published March 1700

'TIS with a Poet, as with a man who designs to build, and is very exact, as he supposes, in casting up the cost beforehand ; but, generally speaking, he is mistaken in his account, and reckons short of the expense he first intended. He alters his mind as the work proceeds, and will have this or that convenience more, of which he had not thought when he began. So has it happened to me ; I have built a house, where I intended but a lodge ; yet with better success than a certain nobleman, who, begin-
10 ning with a dog-kennel, never lived to finish the palace he had contrived.

From translating the First of Homer's *Iliads*, (which I intended as an essay to the whole work,) I proceeded to the translation of the Twelfth Book of Ovid's *Meta-morphoses*, because it contains, among other things, the causes, the beginning, and ending, of the Trojan war. Here I ought in reason to have stopped ; but the speeches of Ajax and Ulysses lying next in my way, I could not balk them. When I had compassed them, I was so taken
20 with the former part of the Fifteenth Book, (which is the masterpiece of the whole *Metamorphoses*,) that I enjoined myself the pleasing task of rendering it into English. And now I found, by the number of my verses, that they began to swell into a little volume ; which gave me an occasion of looking backward on some beauties of my author, in his former books : there occurred to me the Hunting of the Boar, Cinyras and Myrrha, the good-natured story of Baucis and Philemon, with the rest, which I hope I have translated closely enough, and given them the same turn
30 of verse which they had in the original ; and this, I may

say, without vanity, is not the talent of every poet. He
who has arrived the nearest to it, is the ingenious and
learned Sandys, the best versifier of the former age ; if
I may properly call it by that name, which was the former
part of this concluding century. For Spenser and Fairfax
both flourished in the reign of Queen Elizabeth ; great
masters in our language, and who saw much farther into
the beauties of our numbers than those who immediately
followed them. Milton was the poetical son of Spenser,
and Mr. Waller of Fairfax ; for we have our lineal descents 10
and clans as well as other families. Spenser more than once
insinuates, that the soul of Chaucer was transfused into
his body ; and that he was begotten by him two hundred
years after his decease. Milton has acknowledged to me,
that Spenser was his original ; and many besides myself
have heard our famous Waller own, that he derived the
harmony of his numbers from *Godfrey of Bulloign*, which
was turned into English by Mr. Fairfax.

But to return : having done with Ovid for this time,
it came into my mind, that our old English poet, Chaucer, 20
in many things resembled him, and that with no disadvan-
tage on the side of the modern author, as I shall endeavour
to prove when I compare them ; and as I am, and always
have been, studious to promote the honour of my native
country, so I soon resolved to put their merits to the trial,
by turning some of the *Canterbury Tales* into our language,
as it is now refined ; for by this means both the poets
being set in the same light, and dressed in the same English
habit, story to be compared with story, a certain judgment
may be made betwixt them by the reader, without obtrud- 30
ing my opinion on him. Or if I seem partial to my
countryman, and predecessor in the laurel, the friends
of antiquity are not few ; and, besides many of the learned,
Ovid has almost all the *Beaux*, and the whole Fair Sex,
his declared patrons. Perhaps I have assumed somewhat

more to myself than they allow me, because I have adven-
tured to sum up the evidence ; but the readers are the
jury, and their privilege remains entire, to decide according
to the merits of the cause ; or, if they please to bring it
to another hearing, before some other court. In the mean
time, to follow the thrid of my discourse (as thoughts,
according to Mr. Hobbes, have always some connexion),
so from Chaucer I was led to think on Boccace, who was
not only his contemporary, but also pursued the same
10 studies ; wrote novels in prose, and many works in verse ;
particularly is said to have invented the octave rhyme,
or stanza of eight lines, which ever since has been maintained by the practice of all Italian writers who are or at
least assume the title of heroic poets. He and Chaucer,
among other things, had this in common, that they
refined their mother-tongues ; but with this difference,
that Dante had begun to file their language, at least in
verse, before the time of Boccace, who likewise received
no little help from his master Petrarch ; but the reforma-
20 tion of their prose was wholly owing to Boccace himself,
who is yet the standard of purity in the Italian tongue,
though many of his phrases are become obsolete, as in
process of time it must needs happen. Chaucer (as you
have formerly been told by our learned Mr. Rymer) first
adorned and amplified our barren tongue from the Provençal, which was then the most polished of all the modern
languages ; but this subject has been copiously treated
by that great critic, who deserves no little commendation
from us his countrymen. For these reasons of time, and
30 resemblance of genius, in Chaucer and Boccace, I resolved
to join them in my present work ; to which I have added
some original papers of my own, which whether they are
equal or inferior to my other poems, an author is the most
improper judge ; and therefore I leave them wholly to
the mercy of the reader. I will hope the best, that they

will not be condemned ; but if they should, I have the
excuse of an old gentleman, who, mounting on horseback
before some ladies, when I was present, got up somewhat
heavily, but desired of the fair spectators, that they would
count fourscore and eight before they judged him. By the
mercy of God, I am already come within twenty years of
his number, a cripple in my limbs, but what decays are
in my mind, the reader must determine. I think myself
as vigorous as ever in the faculties of my soul, excepting
only my memory, which is not impaired to any great 10
degree ; and if I lose not more of it, I have no great reason
to complain. What judgment I had, increases rather than
diminishes ; and thoughts, such as they are, come crowding
in so fast upon me, that my only difficulty is to choose
or to reject, to run them into verse, or to give them the
other harmony of prose : I have so long studied and
practised both, that they are grown into a habit, and
become familiar to me. In short, though I may lawfully
plead some part of the old gentleman's excuse, yet I will
reserve it till I think I have greater need, and ask no grains 20
of allowance for the faults of this my present work, but
those which are given of course to human frailty. I will
not trouble my reader with the shortness of time in which
I writ it, or the several intervals of sickness. They who
think too well of their own performances, are apt to boast
in their prefaces how little time their works have cost
them, and what other business of more importance inter-
fered ; but the reader will be as apt to ask the question,
why they allowed not a longer time to make their works
more perfect ? and why they had so despicable an opinion 30
of their judges as to thrust their indigested stuff upon them,
as if they deserved no better ?

   With this account of my present undertaking, I conclude the first part of this discourse : in the second part,
as at a second sitting, though I alter not the draught,

I must touch the same features over again, and change
the dead-colouring of the whole. In general I will only
say, that I have written nothing which savours of immorality or profaneness ; at least, I am not conscious to
myself of any such intention. If there happen to be
found an irreverent expression, or a thought too wanton,
they are crept into my verses through my inadvertency :
if the searchers find any in the cargo, let them be staved
or forfeited, like counterbanded goods ; at least, let their
10 authors be answerable for them, as being but imported
merchandise, and not of my own manufacture. On the
other side, I have endeavoured to choose such fables,
both ancient and modern, as contain in each of them some
instructive moral, which I could prove by induction,
but the way is tedious ; and they leap foremost into sight,
without the reader's trouble of looking after them. I wish
I could affirm with a safe conscience, that I had taken the
same care in all my former writings ; for it must be
owned, that supposing verses are never so beautiful or
20 pleasing, yet, if they contain anything which shocks
religion or good manners, they are at best what Horace
says of good numbers without good sense, *Versus inopes
rerum, nugæque canoræ.* Thus far, I hope, I am right in
court, without renouncing to my other right of self-
defence, where I have been wrongfully accused, and my
sense wire-drawn into blasphemy or bawdry, as it has often
been by a religious lawyer, in a late pleading against the
stage ; in which he mixes truth with falsehood, and has
not forgotten the old rule of calumniating strongly, that
30 something may remain.

I resume the thrid of my discourse with the first of my
translations, which was the first *Iliad* of Homer. If it
shall please God to give me longer life, and moderate
health, my intentions are to translate the whole *Ilias* ;
provided still that I meet with those encouragements

from the public, which may enable me to proceed in my undertaking with some cheerfulness. And this I dare assure the world beforehand, that I have found by trial Homer a more pleasing task than Virgil, though I say not the translation will be less laborious. For the Grecian is more according to my genius than the Latin poet. In the works of the two authors we may read their manners, and natural inclinations, which are wholly different. Virgil was of a quiet, sedate temper ; Homer was violent, impetuous, and full of fire. The chief talent of Virgil 10 was propriety of thoughts, and ornament of words : Homer was rapid in his thoughts, and took all the liberties, both of numbers and of expressions, which his language, and the age in which he lived, allowed him. . . . This vehemence of his, I confess, is more suitable to my temper ; and therefore I have translated his First Book with greater pleasure than any part of Virgil ; but it was not a pleasure without pains. The continual agitations of the spirits must needs be a weakening of any constitution, especially in age ; and many pauses are required for refreshment betwixt 20 the heats ; the *Iliad* of itself being a third part longer than all Virgil's works together.

This is what I thought needful in this place to say of Homer. I proceed to Ovid and Chaucer ; considering the former only in relation to the latter. With Ovid ended the golden age of the Roman tongue ; from Chaucer the purity of the English tongue began. The manners of the poets were not unlike. Both of them were well-bred, well-natured, amorous, and libertine, at least in their writings, it may be also in their lives. Their studies were the same, 30 philosophy and philology. Both of them were knowing in astronomy ; of which Ovid's books of the Roman Feasts, and Chaucer's treatise of the Astrolabe, are sufficient witnesses. But Chaucer was likewise an astrologer, as were Virgil, Horace, Persius, and Manilius. Both writ with won-

derful facility and clearness ; neither were great inventors :
for Ovid only copied the Grecian fables, and most of
Chaucer's stories were taken from his Italian contemporaries, or their predecessors. Boccace his *Decameron*
was first published, and from thence our Englishman has
borrowed many of his *Canterbury Tales* : yet that of
Palamon and Arcite was written in all probability by
some Italian wit, in a former age, as I shall prove hereafter.
The tale of Grizild was the invention of Petrarch ; by him
10 sent to Boccace, from whom it came to Chaucer. *Troilus
and Cressida* was also written by a Lombard author, but
much amplified by our English translator, as well as
beautified ; the genius of our countrymen in general
being rather to improve an invention than to invent
themselves, as is evident not only in our poetry, but in
many of our manufactures. I find I have anticipated
already, and taken up from Boccace before I come to him :
but there is so much less behind ; and I am of the temper
of most kings, *who love to be in debt,* are all for present
20 money, no matter how they pay it afterwards : besides,
the nature of a preface is rambling, never wholly out of
the way, nor in it. This I have learned from the practice
of honest Montaigne, and return at my pleasure to Ovid
and Chaucer, of whom I have little more to say.

Both of them built on the inventions of other men ,
yet since Chaucer had something of his own, as *The Wife
of Bath's Tale, The Cock and the Fox,* which I have translated, and some others, I may justly give our countryman
the precedence in that part ; since I can remember
30 nothing of Ovid which was wholly his. Both of them
understood the manners ; under which name I comprehend the passions, and, in a larger sense, the descriptions
of persons, and their very habits. For an example, I see
Baucis and Philemon as perfectly before me, as if some
ancient painter had drawn them ; and all the Pilgrims

in the *Canterbury Tales*, their humours, their features, and the very dress, as distinctly as if I had supped with them at the Tabard in Southwark. Yet even there too the figures of Chaucer are much more lively, and set in a better light ; which though I have not time to prove, yet I appeal to the reader, and am sure he will clear me from partiality. The thoughts and words remain to be considered, in the comparison of the two poets, and I have saved myself one-half of the labour, by owning that Ovid lived when the Roman tongue was in its meridian ; Chaucer, in the dawning of our language : therefore that part of the comparison stands not on an equal foot, any more than the diction of Ennius and Ovid, or of Chaucer and our present English. The words are given up as a post not to be defended in our poet, because he wanted the modern art of fortifying. The thoughts remain to be considered : and they are to be measured only by their propriety ; that is, as they flow more or less naturally from the persons described, on such and such occasions. The vulgar judges, which are nine parts in ten of all nations, who call conceits and jingles wit, who see Ovid full of them, and Chaucer altogether without them, will think me little less than mad for preferring the Englishman to the Roman. Yet, with their leave, I must presume to say, that the things they admire are only glittering trifles, and so far from being witty, that in a serious poem they are nauseous, because they are unnatural. Would any man who is ready to die for love describe his passion like Narcissus ? Would he think of *inopem me copia fecit*, and a dozen more of such expressions, poured on the neck of one another, and signifying all the same thing ? If this were wit, was this a time to be witty, when the poor wretch was in the agony of death ? This is just John Littlewit in *Bartholomew Fair*, who had a conceit (as he tells you) left him in his misery ; a miserable conceit. On these occasions the poet should endeavour to raise pity ; but, instead of this, Ovid is tickling you to laugh. Virgil never made use of such machines when he was moving you to commiserate the death of Dido : he would not destroy what he was building. Chaucer makes Arcite violent in his love, and unjust in the pursuit of it ; yet, when he came to die, he made him think more reasonably : he repents not of his love, for that had altered his character ; but acknowledges the injustice of his proceedings, and resigns Emilia to 10 Palamon. What would Ovid have done on this occasion ? He would certainly have made Arcite witty on his death-bed ; he had complained he was further off from possession, by being so near, and a thousand such boyisms, which Chaucer rejected as below the dignity of the subject. They who think otherwise, would, by the same reason, prefer Lucan and Ovid to Homer and Virgil, and Martial to all four of them. As for the turn of words, in which Ovid particularly excels all poets, they are sometimes a fault, and sometimes a beauty, as they are used properly 20 or improperly ; but in strong passions always to be shunned, because passions are serious, and will admit no playing. The French have a high value for them ; and, I confess, they are often what they call delicate, when they are introduced with judgment ; but Chaucer writ with more simplicity, and followed Nature more closely, than to use them. I have thus far, to the best of my knowledge, been an upright judge betwixt the parties in competition, not meddling with the design nor the disposition of it ; because the design was not their own ; 30 and in the disposing of it they were equal. It remains that I say somewhat of Chaucer in particular.

In the first place, as he is the father of English poetry, so I hold him in the same degree of veneration as the Grecians held Homer, or the Romans Virgil. He is a perpetual fountain of good sense ; learn'd in all sciences ;

and, therefore, speaks properly on all subjects. As he knew what to say, so he knows also when to leave off ; a continence which is practised by few writers, and scarcely by any of the ancients, excepting Virgil and Horace. One of our late great poets is sunk in his reputation, because he could never forgive any conceit which came in his way ; but swept like a drag-net, great and small. There was plenty enough, but the dishes were ill sorted ; whole pyramids of sweetmeats, for boys and women ; but little of solid meat, for men. All this proceeded not from any want of knowledge, but of judgment ; neither did he want that in discerning the beauties and faults of other poets, but only indulged himself in the luxury of writing ; and perhaps knew it was a fault, but hoped the reader would not find it. For this reason, though he must always be thought a great poet, he is no longer esteemed a good writer ; and for ten impressions, which his works have had in so many successive years, yet at present a hundred books are scarcely purchased once a twelvemonth ; for, as my last Lord Rochester said, though somewhat profanely, *Not being of God, he could not stand.*

Chaucer followed Nature everywhere, but was never so bold to go beyond her ; and there is a great difference of being *poeta* and *nimis poeta*, if we may believe Catullus, as much as betwixt a modest behaviour and affectation. The verse of Chaucer, I confess, is not harmonious to us ; but 'tis like the eloquence of one whom Tacitus commends, it was *auribus istius temporis accommodata* : they who lived with him, and some time after him, thought it musical ; and it continues so even in our judgment, if compared with the numbers of Lidgate and Gower, his contemporaries : there is the rude sweetness of a Scotch tune in it, which is natural and pleasing, though not perfect. 'Tis true, I cannot go so far as he who published the last edition of him ; for he would make us believe the

fault is in our ears, and that there were really ten syllables
in a verse where we find but nine : but this opinion is not
worth confuting ; 'tis so gross and obvious an error, that
common sense (which is a rule in everything but matters of
Faith and Revelation) must convince the reader, that
equality of numbers, in every verse which we call *heroic*,
was either not known, or not always practised, in Chaucer's
age. It were an easy matter to produce some thousands
of his verses, which are lame for want of half a foot, and
10 sometimes a whole one, and which no pronunciation can
make otherwise. We can only say, that he lived in the
infancy of our poetry, and that nothing is brought to perfection at the first. We must be children before we grow
men. There was an Ennius, and in process of time a
Lucilius, and a Lucretius, before Virgil and Horace ; even
after Chaucer there was a Spenser, a Harington, a Fairfax,
before Waller and Denham were in being ; and our
numbers were in their nonage till these last appeared. . . .

He must have been a man of a most wonderful com-
20 prehensive nature, because, as it has been truly observed
of him, he has taken into the compass of his *Canterbury
Tales* the various manners and humours (as we now call
them) of the whole English nation, in his age. Not a single
character has escaped him. All his pilgrims are severally
distinguished from each other ; and not only in their
inclinations, but in their very physiognomies and persons.
Baptista Porta could not have described their natures
better, than by the marks which the poet gives them.
The matter and manner of their tales, and of their telling,
30 are so suited to their different educations, humours, and
callings, that each of them would be improper in any other
mouth. Even the grave and serious characters are distinguished by their several sorts of gravity : their discourses
are such as belong to their age, their calling, and their
breeding ; such as are becoming of them, and of them only.

Some of his persons are vicious, and some virtuous ; some
are unlearn'd, or (as Chaucer calls them) lewd, and some
are learn'd.   Even the ribaldry of the low characters is
different : the Reeve, the Miller, and the Cook, are several
men, and distinguished from each other as much as the
mincing Lady-Prioress and the broad-speaking, gap-toothed
Wife of Bath.   But enough of this ; there is such a variety
of game springing up before me, that I am distracted in
my choice, and know not which to follow.   'Tis sufficient
to say according to the proverb, that here is God's plenty. 10
We have our forefathers and great-grand-dames all before
us, as they were in Chaucer's days ; their general characters
are still remaining in mankind, and even in England, though
they are called by other names than those of Monks, and
Friars, and Canons, and Lady Abbesses, and Nuns ;
for mankind is ever the same, and nothing lost out of
Nature, though everything is altered.   May I have leave
to do myself the justice (since my enemies will do me none,
and are so far from granting me to be a good poet, that
they will not allow me so much as to be a Christian, or 20
a moral man), may I have leave, I say, to inform my
reader, that I have confined my choice to such tales of
Chaucer as savour nothing of immodesty.   If I had desired
more to please than to instruct, the Reeve, the Miller,
the Shipman, the Merchant, the Sumner, and, above all,
the Wife of Bath, in the *Prologue* to her *Tale*, would have
procured me as many friends and readers, as there are
beaux and ladies of pleasure in the town.   But I will no
more offend against good manners :   I am sensible as
I ought to be of the scandal I have given by my loose 30
writings ; and make what reparation I am able, by this
public acknowledgment.   If anything of this nature, or
of profaneness, be crept into these poems, I am so far from
defending it, that I disown it.   *Totum hoc indictum volo.*
Chaucer makes another manner of apology for his broad

speaking, and Boccace makes the like ; but I will follow
neither of them.   Our countryman, in the end of his
Characters, before the *Canterbury Tales*, thus excuses the
ribaldry, which is very gross, in many of his novels :

> *But firste, I pray you, of your courtesy,*
> *That ye ne arrete it nought my villany,*
> *Though that I plainly speak in this mattere,*
> *To tellen you her words, and eke her chere :*
> *Ne though I speak her words properly,*
> *For this ye known as well as I,*
> *Who shall tellen a tale after a man,*
> *He mote rehearse as nye as ever he can :*
> *Everich word of it ben in his charge,*
> All spoke he, never so rudely, ne large :
> *Or else he mote tellen his tale untrue,*
> *Or feine things, or find words new :*
> *He may not spare, altho he were his brother,*
> *He mote as wel say o word as another.*
> Crist *spake himself ful broad in holy Writ,*
> *And well I wote no Villany is it.*
> *Eke* Plato *saith, who so can him rede,*
> *The words mote been Cousin to the dede.*

10 (line number)
20 (line number)

Yet if a man should have enquired of Boccace or of
Chaucer, what need they had of introducing such characters, where obscene words were proper in their mouths,
but very undecent to be heard ; I know not what answer
they could have made ; for that reason, such tales shall
be left untold by me.   You have here a *specimen* of
Chaucer's language, which is so obsolete, that his sense
is scarce to be understood ; and you have likewise more
than one example of his unequal numbers, which were
mentioned before.   Yet many of his verses consist of ten
syllables, and the words not much behind our present
English : as for example, these two lines, in the description of the Carpenter's young wife :

> *Wincing she was, as is a jolly Colt,*
> *Long as a Mast, and upright as a Bolt.*

I have almost done with Chaucer, when I have answered some objections relating to my present work. I find some people are offended that I have turned these tales into modern English ; because they think them unworthy of my pains, and look on Chaucer as a dry, old-fashioned wit, not worth reviving. I have often heard the late Earl of Leicester say, that Mr. Cowley himself was of that opinion ; who, having read him over at my Lord's request, declared he had no taste of him. I dare not advance my opinion against the judgment of so great an author ; but I think it fair, however, to leave the decision to the public. Mr. Cowley was too modest to set up for a dictator ; and being shocked perhaps with his old style, never examined into the depth of his good sense. Chaucer, I confess, is a rough diamond, and must first be polished ere he shines. I deny not likewise, that, living in our early days of poetry, he writes not always of a piece, but sometimes mingles trivial things with those of greater moment. Sometimes also, though not often, he runs riot, like Ovid, and knows not when he has said enough. But there are more great wits besides Chaucer, whose fault is their excess of conceits, and those ill sorted. An author is not to write all he can, but only all he ought. Having observed this redundancy in Chaucer, (as it is an easy matter for a man of ordinary parts to find a fault in one of greater,) I have not tied myself to a literal translation ; but have often omitted what I judged unnecessary, or not of dignity enough to appear in the company of better thoughts. I have presumed farther in some places, and added somewhat of my own where I thought my author was deficient, and had not given his thoughts their true lustre, for want of words in the beginning of our language. And to this I was the more emboldened, because (if I may be permitted to say it of myself) I found I had a soul congenial to his, and that

I had been conversant in the same studies. Another poet, in another age, may take the same liberty with my writings ; if at least they live long enough to deserve correction. It was also necessary sometimes to restore the sense of Chaucer, which was lost or mangled in the errors of the press. Let this example suffice at present : in the story of *Palamon and Arcite*, where the temple of Diana is described, you find these verses, in all the editions of our author :

10   *There saw I* Danè *turned unto a tree,*
       I mean not the goddess Diane,
       But Venus *daughter, which that hight* Danè.

Which, after a little consideration, I knew was to be reformed into this sense, that Daphne the daughter of Peneus was turned into a tree. I durst not make thus bold with Ovid, lest some future Milbourne should arise, and say, I varied from my author, because I understood him not.

But there are other judges who think I ought not to
20 have translated Chaucer into English, out of a quite con-
trary notion : they suppose there is a certain veneration due to his old language ; and that it is little less than profanation and sacrilege to alter it. They are farther of opinion, that somewhat of his good sense will suffer in this transfusion, and much of the beauty of his thoughts will infallibly be lost, which appear with more grace in their old habit. Of this opinion was that excellent person whom I mentioned, the late Earl of Leicester, who valued Chaucer as much as Mr. Cowley despised him.
30 My Lord dissuaded me from this attempt, (for I was thinking of it some years before his death,) and his authority prevailed so far with me, as to defer my undertaking while he lived, in deference to him : yet my reason was not convinced with what he urged against it. If the first

end of a writer be to be understood, then, as his language grows obsolete, his thoughts must grow obscure ;

> *Multa renascentur, quæ nunc cecidere ; cadentque*
> *Quæ nunc sunt in honore vocabula, si volet usus,*
> *Quem penes arbitrium est et jus et norma loquendi.*

When an ancient word for its sound and significancy deserves to be revived, I have that reasonable veneration for antiquity to restore it. All beyond this is superstition. Words are not like landmarks, so sacred as never to be removed ; customs are changed, and even statutes are 10 silently repealed, when the reason ceases for which they were enacted. As for the other part of the argument, that his thoughts will lose of their original beauty by the innovation of words ; in the first place, not only their beauty, but their being is lost, where they are no longer understood, which is the present case. I grant that something must be lost in all transfusion, that is, in all translations ; but the sense will remain, which would otherwise be lost, or at least be maimed, when it is scarce intelligible, and that but to a few. How few are there who 20 can read Chaucer, so as to understand him perfectly ? And if imperfectly, then with less profit, and no pleasure. 'Tis not for the use of some old Saxon friends, that I have taken these pains with him : let them neglect my version, because they have no need of it. I made it for their sakes who understand sense and poetry as well as they, when that poetry and sense is put into words which they understand. I will go farther, and dare to add, that what beauties I lose in some places, I give to others which had them not originally ; but in this I may be partial to myself ; 30 let the reader judge, and I submit to his decision. Yet I think I have just occasion to complain of them, who because they understand Chaucer, would deprive the greater part of their countrymen of the same advantage, and

hoard him up, as misers do their grandam gold, only to
look on it themselves, and hinder others from making use
of it.   In sum, I seriously protest, that no man ever had,
or can have, a greater veneration for Chaucer than myself.
I have translated some part of his works, only that I might
perpetuate his memory, or at least refresh it, amongst my
countrymen.   If I have altered him anywhere for the better,
I must at the same time acknowledge, that I could have
done nothing without him.   *Facile est inventis addere* is no
10 great commendation ; and I am not so vain to think I have
deserved a greater.   I will conclude what I have to say of
him singly, with this one remark : A lady of my acquaintance, who keeps a kind of correspondence with some authors
of the fair sex in France, has been informed by them, that
Mademoiselle de Scudéry, who is as old as Sibyl, and
inspired like her by the same God of Poetry, is at this time
translating Chaucer into modern French.   From which
I gather, that he has been formerly translated into the old
Provençal ; for how she should come to understand old
20 English, I know not.   But the matter of fact being true, it
makes me think that there is something in it like fatality ;
that, after certain periods of time, the fame and memory of
great Wits should be renewed, as Chaucer is both in France
and England.   If this be wholly chance, 'tis extraordinary ;
and I dare not call it more, for fear of being taxed with
superstition. . . .

NOTES

CONGREVE'S DEDICATION

See Dryden's Epistle *To My Dear Friend Mr. Congreve*, pp. 110–12, and especially the closing lines where Dryden adjures Congreve to be kind to his remains and to protect his fame from the insulting foe. In fulfilling the duty thus imposed on him, Congreve gave us the only authentic ' character ' of Dryden written by a contemporary, and the first judicial estimate of Dryden's work as a whole.

JOHNSON'S LIFE

PAGE **4,** l. 9. *The dialogue on the Drama*, the essay *Of Dramatic Poesy*, 1668 : see pp. 143–52.

l. 20. *The account of Shakespeare*, p. 150.

l. 23. *Longinus,—On the Sublime*, xvi.

PAGE **6,** l. 9. *His conversation*, &c. *Threnodia Augustalis*, 1685, ll. 337–45.

PAGE **8,** l. 35. *Ben Jonson*, in his translation of the *Ars Poetica* and of three of Horace's Odes.

PAGE **9,** l. 1. *Feltham*, or Felltham, Owen (1602–68), best known as the author of *Resolves*, wrote *An Answer to the Ode of Come leave the loathed Stage* by Jonson, in which he says :

> 'Tis known you can do well,
> And that you do excell
> As a Translator. (*Lusoria*, 1616, No. xx.)

In his *Resolves* the Latin quotations are followed by English renderings in the same number of lines.

l. 3. *Sandys*. See p. 161, l. 3, and note.

l. 7. *Holyday*. See p. 158, l. 4, and note.

l. 12. *Cowley*. See the Preface to his *Pindaric Odes* : ' . . . exact *Imitation* ; which being a vile and unworthy kind of *Servitude*, is incapable of producing any thing good or noble.' But Johnson has also Horace in mind, Epistles I, xix. 19, ' O imitatores, servum pecus '.

l. 24. *says Dryden*, in the ' Dedication of the Aeneis ', 1697 : ' The way I have taken is not so strait as metaphrase, nor so loose as paraphrase ' (ed. W. P. Ker, ii. 227). Elsewhere he defines *metaphrase* as ' turning an author word by word, and line by line, from one language into another ' (Preface to Ovid's Epistles, 1680, *Essays of Dryden*, ed. W. P. Ker, i. 237).

PAGE **10**, l. 17. *What had been*, &c. *Don Sebastian*, **iv.** iii. *ad fin.*

PAGE **12**, l. 25. *Henceforth*, &c. See p. 79, l. 1028.

PAGE **13**, ll. 20, 21. *And this unpolish'd*, &c. See p. 90, ll. 453, 454.

PAGE **15**, l. 5. *Stapylton.* See p. 158, l. 17, and note.

l. 19. *Creech*, Thomas (1659–1700), translator of Lucretius, Horace, &c.

l. 22. *some passages excepted.* Johnson must have had in mind the opening of Satire X,—which he himself imitated in *The Vanity of Human Wishes.* See p. 112.

PAGE **16**, l. 16. *says Pope*, in the Preface to his translation of the *Iliad* : ' It is a great Loss to the Poetical World that Mr. *Dryden* did not live to translate the *Iliad* . . . had he translated the whole *Work*, I would no more have attempted *Homer* after him than *Virgil*, his Version of whom (notwithstanding some human Errors) is the most noble and spirited Translation I know in any Language.'

l. 23. *new attempts*, notably the translation by Christopher Pitt (1699–1748), whose life is included in the *Lives of the Poets.* Johnson there calls Dryden's *Aeneid* and Pitt's ' the two best translations that perhaps were ever produced by one nation of the same author ', and gives a brief comparison of their merits : ' Dryden leads the reader forward by his general vigour and sprightliness, and Pitt often stops him to contemplate the excellence of a single couplet . . . Pitt pleases the critics, and Dryden the people . . . Pitt is quoted, and Dryden read.'

PAGE **17**, l. 18. *the old poem of Boiardo*, the *Orlando Innamorato*, ' nuovamente composto ', by Francesco Berni, 1541, and ' nuovamente riformato ', by Lodovico Domenichi, 1545.

l. 34. *one of the Beroalds*, Filippo Beroaldo the elder (1453–1505), of Bologna. His Latin translation was published about 1495.

PAGE **18**, l. 5. *Congreve's remark.* See p. 3, ll. 20–3.

l. 9. *Ode for St. Cecilia's Day*, i. e. *Alexander's Feast.*

PAGE **19**, l. 13. *Love various minds*, &c. *Tyrannic Love*, Act II. *ad fin.* The original has ' gentle Natures '.

l. 32. *Otway.* See Dryden's *Parallel of Poetry and Painting*, 1695 : ' I will not defend everything in his *Venice Preserved* ; but I must bear this testimony to his memory, that the passions are truly touched in it, though perhaps there is somewhat to be desired, both in the grounds of them, and in the height and elegance of expression ; but nature is there, which is the greatest beauty ' (*Essays*, ed. W. P. Ker, ii. 145). Charles Gildon in his *Laws of Poetry*, 1721, p. 211, says of Dryden that ' for most part of his time he commonly express'd a very mean if not contemptible opinion of Otway ' ; and

Robert Shiels in his life of Otway in Cibber's *Lives of the Poets*, 1753, ii. 332, reports that ' Dryden was often heard to say that Otway was a barren illiterate man, but " I confess ", says he, " he has a power which I have not " ; and when it was asked him what power that was, he answered, " moving the passions ".'

PAGE 20, l. 21. *Verbaque provisam rem non invita sequentur*, Horace, *Ars Poetica*, l. 311.

PAGE 21, l. 3. *Dalilahs*. See the Dedication of the *Spanish Friar* 1681 : ' All I can say for those passages, which are, I hope, not many, is that I knew they were bad enough to please, even when I writ them ; but I repent of them amongst my sins ; and if any of their fellows intrude by chance into my present writings, I draw a stroke over all those Delilahs of the Theatre, and am resolved I will settle myself no reputation by the applause of fools ' (ed. W. P. Ker, i. 246).

PAGE 21, l. 33. *no example of any correction*. This is put too strongly. Dryden revised his essay *Of Dramatic Poesy* and *Absalom and Achitophel*.

PAGE 22, l. 5. *Waller was smooth*, Pope, *Epistle to Augustus*, ll. 267-9.

l. 16. *said by Pope*. He is reported by Joseph Spence to have said ' I learned versification wholly from Dryden's works : who had improved it much beyond any of our former poets ' (Spence's *Anecdotes*, ed. Singer, p. 281). Cf. Congreve, p. 2, ll. 15, 16.

l. 23. *sapere et fari*, Horace, *Epistles* I. iv. 9.

l. 24. *Davies*, Sir John (1569-1626), author of *Nosce teipsum*.

l. 30. *lateritiam*, &c., Suetonius, Augustus XXIX : ' marmoream se relinquere quam lateritiam accepisset '.

SCOTT'S LIFE

PAGE 24, l. 3. *Sebastian and Dorax,—Don Sebastian* IV. iii.

PAGE 28, l. 2. *the ' old Saxon ' admirers of Chaucer*, an awkward rendering of Dryden's words, p. 175, l. 23.

HAZLITT'S LECTURE

PAGE 30, l. 15. *Ode on St. Cecilia*, i. e. *Alexander's Feast*.

PAGE 31, l. 12. *The Flower and the Leaf*, a fifteenth-century poem included in the older editions of Chaucer's works, and commonly believed to be his till the middle of the nineteenth century : see Skeat's *Chaucer*, vol. vii (*Chaucerian Pieces*), pp. 360-79. Skeat says that it is ' chiefly famous for having been versified by Dryden. The version is a free one, in a manner all his own, and is finer than the original '. Most readers are likely to agree with Hazlitt in preferring the old poem ; but Dryden's version has its merits.

l. 18. *Thou gladder*, &c. *The Knight's Tale*, l. 1365.

l. 22. *Isabella.* The fifth tale of the fourth day in Boccaccio's *Decameron.* Hazlitt's lecture (No. IV of his course on the English Poets) was delivered at the beginning of February 1818. Keats attended the course : ' I hear Hazlitt's lectures regularly, his last was on Gray, Collins, Young, &c.' (No. VI), he writes in a letter of Saturday, 21 February 1818. It was in February 1818 that Keats began his *Isabella, or the Pot of Basil.*

the Falcon. The ninth tale of the fifth day in the *Decameron.* It has been often retold, e. g. by Cervantes, by La Fontaine, by Longfellow in *Tales of a Wayside Inn*, and in Tennyson's drama *The Falcon.*

Constance. The Man of Law's Tale.

Hazlitt had learned from Wordsworth, probably in 1803, that he had modernized some of the *Canterbury Tales* (see his essay on Wordsworth in *The Spirit of the Age*), and he must have had Wordsworth in mind when recommending versions of some of Chaucer's serious tales. Wordsworth modernized the Prioress's Tale (written 1801, published 1820), and the Manciple's Tale (unpublished ; see *Memoirs of Wordsworth*, ii. 375).

HEROIC STANZAS

Cromwell died on 3 September 1658, and was buried in Westminster Abbey on 23 November. Dryden's poem was published with poems by Edmund Waller and Thomas Sprat (afterwards Bishop of Rochester) in a pamphlet entitled *Three Poems upon the Death of his late Highness Oliver Lord Protector*, &c. It was his first notable work—the first to show the promise of his mature verse.

The stanza was adopted from Sir William Davenant's long poem *Gondibert*, 1651, and is sometimes called ' the Gondibert stanza ' when used for narrative. Structurally it is the same as the stanza of Gray's *Elegy*.

ll. 11-12. Pompey reached the height of his prosperity on his forty-fifth birthday, on his return to Rome from his Eastern conquests, 61 B. C., then lost the favour of fortune, and was assassinated in Egypt 48 B. C. when entering his fifty-ninth year. Cromwell won the battle of Marston Moor at the age of forty-five, and died at the age of fifty-nine.

l. 21. *those stars*, probably ' St. Elmo's lights ' or corposants, balls of light seen about the masts of a ship during storms ; but ' the height of the storm is commonly over when the *Corpus Sant* is seen aloft ' (Dampier, *Voyage round the World*, 1697, I. xv. 414, quoted in *Oxford English Dictionary*).

l. 25. *His ashes*, &c. The prophecy was not fulfilled : on

30 January 1661, the anniversary of the execution of Charles I, Cromwell's body was removed from Westminster and hung on the gallows at Tyburn. When Dryden wrote this poem Richard Cromwell was expected to maintain his father's power.

ASTRÆA REDUX

Charles II landed at Dover on 26 May 1660, and entered London on 29 May, his birthday. *Astræa* was the goddess of Justice.

This was Dryden's first notable poem in the heroic couplet. The best passages announce the author of *Absalom and Achitophel*.

l. 21. A star appeared at noon on the day of Charles II's birth—29 May 1630. ' There is nothing to support Scott's unnecessary conjecture that the same star was again visible on 29 May 1660. Lilly the astrologer declared the star to be the planet Venus ; and he was doubtless right. Derrick mentions that Venus was similarly seen by day in 1757. It was lately so seen in May, 1868 ' (W. D. Christie, 1871).

l. 29. *edicts.* ' Dryden refers to the King's proclamation against vicious, debauched, and profane persons, issued 30 May 1660, the day after he entered London ' (C. H. Firth).

ANNUS MIRABILIS.

Dryden reverts to the Gondibert stanza, and in his Preface defends his choice of it for a narrative poem. ' I have chosen ', he says, ' to write my poem in quatrains or stanzas of four in alternate rhyme, because I have ever judged them more noble and of greater dignity both for the sound and number than any other verse in use amongst us.' But it was his last poem in this stanza.

The Preface is dated ' From Charlton, in Wiltshire, Nov. 10, 1666 '. Dryden had retired to Charlton to avoid the Plague, and, it would appear, had not seen the Fire. But his description is corroborated by the diaries of Pepys and Evelyn, who both saw it, and who supply the best commentary on the poem.

l. 9. The Fire broke out in the early morning of Sunday, 2 September, and raged for six days. Pepys was called up at three in the morning to see it, and later in the day was told by the Lieutenant of the Tower that it began that morning in the King's baker's house in Pudding Lane (*Diary*, 2 Sept. 1666).

l. 41. *the Bridge,* London Bridge, where by old custom the heads of those executed for treason were exhibited. Cf. Shakespeare, *Richard III*, III. ii. 70 ; and see Visscher's view of London, 1616, which depicts several heads on poles at the south end of the Bridge (reproduced in *Shakespeare's England*, ii. 174).

'The *Sabbath notes* imputed to this assembly of fanatic spectres are the infernal hymns chanted at the witches' Sabbath—a meeting concerning which antiquity told and believed many strange things' (Sir Walter Scott, in a note on 'this most beautiful stanza').

l. 45.   *in a broader gross.*   'In gross' is a military term meaning 'in a body', 'en masse'.

l. 69.   Cf. Evelyn, *Diary*, 6 September : 'It is not indeed imaginable how extraordinary the vigilance and activity of the King and the Duke was, even labouring in person, and being present to command, order, reward, or encourage workmen'.

l. 77.   Cf. Pepys, *Diary*, 4 September : 'Now begins the practice of blowing up of houses in Tower Street, those next the Tower, which at first did frighten people more than anything ; but it stopped the fire where it was done, it bringing down the houses to the ground in the same places they stood, and then it was easy to quench what little fire was in it'. Cf. Evelyn, 5 September.

l. 95.   *retire*, withdrew, take away ; Fr. *retirer.*

l. 98.   *general doom*, the day of judgement.

l. 106.   *require*, Lat. *requirere*, to seek again.

l. 132.   Dryden makes Charles say what David had said in 1 Chronicles xxi. 17 : 'let thine hand, I pray thee, O Lord my God, be on me, and on my father's house ; but not on thy people, that they should be plagued'.

l. 137.   The Plague had begun in the summer of 1665, and was not extinct when the Fire broke out.

l. 152.   Cf. 1 Chronicles xxi. 13.

l. 159.   *a poet's song*, Edmund Waller's poem 'Upon his Majesty's repairing of Paul's', written about 1635.

l. 203.   *the town*, 'Mexico' (note by Dryden).

l. 209.   *Augusta*, 'the old name of London' (note by Dryden). Cf. Pope's *Windsor Forest*, ll. 336 and 377.   Dryden's prophecy anticipates the conclusion of Pope's poem in several points.

'Augusta' is known as the name of London only in the fourth century.   The authorities for it are Ammianus Marcellinus, xxvii. 8. 6 'ad Lundinium vetus oppidum, quod Augustam posteritas appellavit', and xxviii. 3. 1 'ab Augusta profectus quam veteres appellavere Lundinium', and two coins struck at the London mint in the reign of Valentinian. There is no record of the name before Valentinian or after the death of Ammianus Marcellinus in 400.

THE DRAMAS

Dryden wrote dramas for over thirty years, from *The Wild Gallant* in 1663 to *Love Triumphant* in 1694, and in the year of his death he wrote *The Secular Masque*.   But his chief work as a dramatist belongs to the fourteen years between *Annus Mirabilis* and *Absalom and Achitophel* ; and in these years he wrote little else than dramas or dramatic criticism. They cannot be adequately represented in this small book, and his comedies must be entirely neglected ; but all his dramas ought not to be neglected, for some of them played a great part in his poetic development. In his Heroic Plays, dramas of ' love and honour ' all written in rhyme, he perfected himself in the heroic couplet. He wrote five of these plays— *The Indian Emperor, Tyrannic Love, The Conquest of Granada* (2 parts), and *Aureng-zebe*. Whatever may be said against them as dramas, and much may be said, they all contain passages of splendid versification. At the very least they were the training-ground in which he became master of his craft.

PAGE 53, l. 57. *loose*, impulse, rush ; used particularly of horses when given the rein.

PAGE 53. *Aureng-zebe*. These lines were well-known in the eighteenth century. They were frequently quoted by Samuel Johnson. Cf. *The Spectator*, No. 323 : ' Kitty repeated without book the eight best lines in the play '.

PAGE 54. Prologue to *Aureng-zebe*. Dryden had argued for rhyme in his essay *Of Dramatic Poesy*, 1668, and had used it in his Heroic Plays. He now (1676) confesses that he grows weary of rhyme, and ' in a just despair would quit the stage ' when he compares his work with Shakespeare's. His next serious play was to be in blank verse.

ALL FOR LOVE

PAGE 55. ' In my style I have professed to imitate the divine Shakespeare ; which that I might perform more freely, I have disencumbered myself from rhyme. . . . Since I must not be over-confident of my own performance after him, it will be prudent in me to be silent. Yet, I hope, I may affirm, and without vanity, that by imitating him I have excelled myself throughout the play ; and particularly that I prefer the scene betwixt Antony and Ventidius in the first act to anything which I have written in this kind ' (Preface to *All for Love*).

As this passage shows, Dryden had no thought of rivalling ' the divine Shakespeare ' ; he makes the experiment of telling the story of Antony and Cleopatra according to a different dramatic method. The action in Shakespeare's play extends over many years, and the scene is the Mediterranean or the whole civilized world ; in *All for Love* Dryden obeys the strict laws of the three unities and confines the action to one day and one place. His play has therefore to begin immediately before the catastrophe ; his Antony, unlike Shakespeare's, is the Antony of the last day of his life—from the first scene he is a ruined Antony.

Dryden, who is best known for his rhymed couplets, here shows himself to be a master of blank verse. There has been no better dramatic blank verse since Shakespeare's.

All for Love is generally regarded as Dryden's greatest play, though Scott speaks of *Don Sebastian* as ' the *chef-d'œuvre* of Dryden's dramatic works '. Both of these plays, as well as *The Conquest of Granada* and *Aureng-zebe*, are given in the Mermaid edition, ed. Saintsbury.

PAGE **62,** l. 255. *ostentation sake.* The dropping of the genitive ending before *sake* (cf. goodness sake) goes back to the beginning of the fourteenth century.

ABSALOM AND ACHITOPHEL

Charles II had married Catherine of Braganza in 1662, but they had no children. The heir to the throne was Charles's brother, James, Duke of York, and he was a Roman Catholic. The Whig party, under the leadership of the Earl of Shaftesbury, opposed his succession, and supported the Duke of Monmouth, Charles's son by Lucy Walter, a man of great personal charm and a Protestant. They passed the Exclusion Bill (excluding the Duke of York from the throne) in the House of Commons in October 1680, but it was at once rejected in the House of Lords. In July 1681 Shaftesbury was arrested on a charge of high treason and thrown into the Tower to await his trial in November. On 17 November, a week before the trial, Dryden brought out his *Absalom and Achitophel*.

The biblical parallel (2 Samuel xiv–xviii) had suggested itself to others as well as Dryden, and there was no novelty in the main design of his satire. The novelty lay in the brilliant use which Dryden made of his opportunity. His poem is a contribution to a fierce political struggle—a satire on the Whigs, a satire in defence of the Crown ; but it is the only political satire in the language which, written with an immediate purpose, ranks as great literature. It rises above the circumstances out of which it sprang, and lives when these are forgotten. For it is more than a political satire. Minute study of the historical facts may enhance our appreciation of it ; but our interest must always be centred in the skill with which Dryden has presented the ambitions and characters of the principal actors in a great drama.

David is Charles ; Absalom, the Duke of Monmouth ; Achitophel, the Earl of Shaftesbury ; Zimri, the Duke of Buckingham ; the Jews, the English ; the Jebusites, the Roman Catholics ; Israel, England ; Sion, London ; Hebron, Scotland ; the Jordan, the English Channel.

PAGE **66,** l. 11. *Michal*, Catherine of Braganza : cf. 2 Samuel vi. 23.

l. 34. *Annabel*, the Countess of Buccleuch in her own right, married to Monmouth in 1665.

l. 39. *Amnon's murder*, perhaps a reference to the slitting of Sir John Coventry's nose, at Monmouth's instigation, in 1670, in revenge for what he had said in the House of Commons about the king's mistresses ; but no convincing explanation has yet been found.

l. 43. *sincerely*, purely, without alloy ; Lat. *sincerus*.

l. 44. *proves*, tests ; Lat. *probare*.

ll. 51–6. 'An allusion to the " state of nature " which Hobbes and other political writers of the period supposed to have existed before states and commonwealths were founded. In this state of nature all men were equal, and there was no government, but a war of every one against every one else ' (C. H. Firth).

Adam-wits, wits with as little restraint on their liberty as Adam in the Garden of Eden.

l. 57. *Saul*, Oliver Cromwell ; *Ishbosheth*, Richard Cromwell.

l. 134. *This plot*, the alleged Popish Plot to murder the King and put the government in the hands of the Jesuits, invented by Titus Oates, 1678.

ll. 150–97. 'You will find this a good gauge or criterion of genius—whether it progresses and evolves, or only spins upon itself. Take Dryden's Achitophel and Zimri ; every line adds to or modifies the character, which is, as it were, abuilding up to the very last verse.'—Coleridge, *Table Talk*, 6 August 1832.

l. 163. Cf. Seneca, *De Tranquillitate Animi*, xvii. 10 : ' nullum magnum ingenium sine mixtura dementiae fuit '.

l. 170. The humorous definition of man ascribed to Plato in Diogenes Laertius, vi. 40 (Life of Diogenes), ἄνθρωπός ἐστι ζῷον δίπουν ἄπτερον.—The son was a handsomer man than the father, though he did not inherit his ability.

l. 175. *the triple bond*, the alliance of England, Holland, and Sweden against France in 1667, broken by the war with France against Holland in 1672.

ll. 180–91. These twelve lines were added in the second edition. The praise of Shaftesbury's impartiality as a judge heightens the satire on his guilt as a politician. Shaftesbury was Lord Chancellor in 1672–3. *Abbethdin*, the father of the house of judgement.

l. 197. David would have sung his praises instead of writing a psalm, and so Heaven would have had one immortal song the less.

l. 204. *manifest of*, having evident signs of ; Lat. *manifestus* with genitive.

l. 222. Dryden insinuates that Shaftesbury is not so intent on advancing Monmouth as on weakening the Crown, in order to set up a republic over which he should himself preside.

ll. 252 et seq. Cf. *Julius Caesar*, IV. iii. 217 : ' There is a tide in the affairs of men,' &c.

l. 264. *Gath*, Brussels.

l. 270. *Jordan's sand*, the beach at Dover. Cf. *Astræa Redux*, p. 41, ll. 9–24.

ll. 478 et seq. Dryden had to treat Monmouth gently, for the king was fond of him. Moreover his personal charm made him a popular favourite ; and the Duchess was one of Dryden's best patrons. He is therefore painted as the tool of Shaftesbury, and ' lamented ' rather than ' accused '.

ll. 543–68. ' The character of Zimri in my *Absalom* is, in my opinion, worth the whole poem.' See the whole passage in the extracts from Dryden's *Discourse concerning Satire*, pp. 158, 159.

Zimri was the second Duke of Buckingham, the son of Charles I's favourite. He had ridiculed Dryden and his Heroic Plays in *The Rehearsal*, 1672, where he gave Dryden (then poet-laureate) the name of ' John Bayes '.

l. 688. *to show*, on show, *sets to show*, displays—now obsolete ; *show* is a substantive.

ll. 727–736. Monmouth made a progress through Wiltshire, Somerset, and Devon in August 1680. ' He was met at Taunton by near thirty thousand persons, mostly on horseback ' (Sir John Dalrymple's *Memoirs*, 1771, i. 55).

ll. 817—913. Dryden's mastery as a satirist ought not to be allowed to obscure his excellence in friendly portraiture. These slighter sketches of Charles's friends glow with warmth of feeling, and are admirable in the skill with which in a few couplets they describe both character and the parts that had been played.

l. 817. *Barzillai*, James Butler, Duke of Ormond (1610–88), Lord Lieutenant of Ireland at the beginning of the Civil War, and again after the Restoration. From 1651 to 1659 he attended on Charles in exile, or served on embassies for him. He was one of Dryden's patrons.

l. 825. *The court he practised*, i. e. frequented, Fr. *pratiquer*.

l. 877. *Adriel*, John Sheffield, Earl of Mulgrave, afterwards Duke of Buckinghamshire (1648–1721), author of *An Essay on Satire* (in which he is supposed to have had Dryden's assistance), and *An Essay on Poetry*, 1682. His collected works were edited by Pope in 1723, and his life was written by Johnson in the *Lives of the Poets*. Dryden dedicated *Aurengzebe* to him.

l. 878. *Sanhedrin*, parliament.

ll. 880, 881. *honours*. ' The Duke of Monmouth at that time was in such disfavour, as to have his Government at Hull and Lord Lieutenancy of Yorkshire given to me.' Mulgrave's ' Memoirs ', *Works*, ed. 1723, i, p. 20.

l. 882. *Jotham*, George Savile, Marquis of Halifax (1633–95),

author of *The Character of a Trimmer* and himself the chief
' Trimmer ', the name given to the moderate men who tried to
' trim ' the political boat. He was not on good terms with
James, but he secured the rejection of the Exclusion Bill in
the House of Lords. ' Halifax employs the subtlest resources
of wit in defence of the practical expedient, the middle course,
the reasonable compromise ' (Walter Raleigh, Introduction to
Works of Savile, 1912).

l. 888. *Hushai*, Laurence Hyde, second son of Lord Chancellor Clarendon, created Viscount Hyde 1680 and Earl of
Rochester 1682 (1641–1711), first lord of the Treasury 1679–85.
He had been ambassador to Poland and a plenipotentiary at
the congress of Nimeguen.

l. 899. *Amiel*, Edward Seymour (1633–1708), afterwards
Sir Edward Seymour, head of the house of Seymour, the then
Duke of Somerset being of a younger branch of the family.
He was Speaker from 1673 to 1679.

l. 910. *the unequal ruler*, &c. Phaethon.

ll. 939 et seq. Pope is reported by Joseph Spence to have
said that ' King Charles obliged Dryden to put his Oxford
speech into verse, and to insert it toward the close of his
Absalom and Achitophel ' (Spence's *Anecdotes*, ed. Singer,
p. 172). But David's speech is far from being a paraphrase of
the speech with which Charles opened the parliament at Oxford
on 21 March 1681. The parts which Malone thought that
Dryden might have had in mind are quoted in his Life of Dryden, *Prose Works*, 1800, i, pp. 154, 155.

ll. 957–60. Added in the second edition, like ll. 180–91.

l. 976. *to give their own*, i. e. to give what is theirs to give.

l. 982. Genesis xxvii. 22.

l. 987. Proverbs xxx. 15, 16.

THE MEDAL

Shaftesbury was freed from the charge of high treason on
24 November 1681, when the Grand Jury threw out the bill
against him, and the Whigs in their exultation struck a medal
in his honour. It bore his bust and name, and on the reverse
a view of London with the sun rising above the Tower and
dispersing a cloud, the date 24 November 1681, and the legend
' Laetamur '.

Charles II is said to have given Dryden the hint for writing
The Medal. ' One day, as the king was walking in the Mall,
and talking with Dryden, he said, " If I was a poet, and I think
I am poor enough to be one, I would write a poem on such
a subject, in the following manner " : and then gave him the
plan for it.—Dryden took the hint, carried the poem as soon

as it was finished to the king, and had a present of a hundred broad pieces for it ' (Spence, *Anecdotes*, pp. 171, 172).

The poem is another satire on Shaftesbury, less playful, and more bitter ; but it is also a satire on the folly of the crowd that allows itself to be duped by the seditious acts of the clever politician. Dryden saw that the English character ' will no extremes sustain ' (l. 248).

PAGE **80,** ll. 50 et seq. Shaftesbury had joined the Parliamentarians in 1644, but he negotiated with Charles in March 1660, was raised to the peerage as Baron Ashley in 1661, and was Chancellor of the Exchequer from 1661 to 1672, when he became Lord Chancellor and was raised to his Earldom. He was dismissed in 1673 and joined the Whig party.

l. 94. A ' Pindaric ' line of fourteen syllables. See note on ' Pindaric verse ', p. 191.

MACFLECKNOE

The title of the first edition runs thus : *MacFlecknoe. Or a Satyr upon the True-Blew-Protestant Poet, T. S. By the Author of Absalom and Achitophel. London, Printed for D. Green,* 1682. All that is known of D. Green is that he published in the same year *MacFlecknoe* and the second issue of an attack on Dryden entitled *Satyr to his Muse. By the Author of Absalom and Achitophel* (the first issue was ' Printed for T. W. 1682 '). He was not one of Dryden's regular publishers, and the text of his edition of *MacFlecknoe* is very faulty. There is reason to believe that the poem was known in manuscript for some time before it was published. Green, it would appear, acquired a copy and printed it without Dryden's knowledge.

The poem was printed with the simple title *MacFlecknoe* in 1684 in the volume entitled *Miscellany Poems . . . By the most Eminent Hands,* afterwards known as the first volume of ' Dryden's Miscellany Poems '. The text of this edition is good, and all later texts have been based on it. This is the first edition with a good claim to be called authorized.

The occasion of *MacFlecknoe,* the date of composition, and the date of publication are all problems. Since 1800, when Malone brought out his Life of Dryden (prefixed to his edition of the *Prose Works*), it has been regularly stated to be a reply to *The Medal of John Bayes,* a coarse personal attack on Dryden written in answer to *The Medal* and assumed to be by Thomas Shadwell. Advertisements show that *The Medal of John Bayes* was published in May 1682. There are no advertisements of *MacFlecknoe* in 1682, but Malone asserted that it was published on 4 October, and this is the date that has been generally accepted since his time. But the following points have to be considered :

(1) Malone probably derived the date from a note written by Narcissus Luttrell on the title-page of his copy of *Mac-Flecknoe*, but 4 October may be only the day of purchase, not also of publication.

(2) Dryden satirized Shadwell in the Second Part of *Absalom and Achitophel*, which appeared on 10 November 1682, and we should not expect him to have written two separate satires on Shadwell at about the same time.

(3) There is no passage in *MacFlecknoe* which was manifestly suggested by anything in *The Medal of John Bayes*, nothing which is necessarily later than May 1682.

(4) There is no evidence that *The Medal of John Bayes* was written by Shadwell. Malone attributed it to him only on the strength of a manuscript note by Luttrell. In no account of Shadwell written by his contemporaries, or during the whole of the eighteenth century, is this poem mentioned or alluded to ; and no support for attributing it to Shadwell is to be found in his reply to Dryden in the Preface to his translation of *The Tenth Satire of Juvenal*, 1687.

(5) As Mr. Thorn Drury has pointed out (*Modern Language Review*, July 1918, p. 280), *The Loyal Protestant* of Thursday, 9 February 1681/2, contains the following passage in the course of an attack on Shadwell : ' he would send him (Shadwell) his Recantation next morning, with a *MacFlecknoe*, and a brace of Lobsters for his Breakfast ; All which he knew he had a singular aversion for '. (Whether ' a *MacFlecknoe* ' means a printed copy, or a manuscript copy, is not clear.)

In view of all this we cannot any longer hold that *Mac-Flecknoe* was written in the summer or early autumn of 1682, or that it was written in retaliation for *The Medal of John Bayes*. The immediate occasion of the satire on Shadwell has yet to be discovered.

Thomas Shadwell (1640–92) had lived on outwardly friendly terms with Dryden. They had collaborated in 1674 in the *Observations* on Settle's *Empress of Morocco*, and as late as 1678 Dryden had provided the Prologue for Shadwell's *True Widow*. Thereafter we know them only as openly hostile. As a writer Shadwell has greater merits than Dryden's satire can allow. His prose comedies, which are modelled on Ben Jonson's, have distinct value as pictures of the times, and they were popular in their own day. But he made the mistake of not confining himself to prose. When he wrote verse even his defenders must admit that he wrote ' doggerel rhymes '. In *MacFlecknoe* Dryden represents Shadwell as the chosen son of Richard Flecknoe, a notorious poetaster who had died about 1678 and of whom the contemporary opinion is well expressed in Langbaine's *Dramatick Poets*, 1691—' His acquaintance with the Nobility was more than with the Muses ; and he had a greater propensity to Riming than a genius to Poetry.' In its description of Shadwell's succession to Flecknoe on the throne of Dulness, *MacFlecknoe* is the direct ancestor of *The Dunciad*.

ABSALOM AND ACHITOPHEL, SECOND PART

The continuation of *Absalom and Achitophel* was written by Nahum Tate, but Dryden revised it and contributed a section of about 250 lines. In this section he satirizes Elkanah Settle, who had written *Absalom Senior* in reply to *Absalom and Achitophel*, and returns to the attack on Shadwell. Settle (Doeg) ' rhymes and rattles ' and Shadwell (Og) ' writes dull '.

RELIGIO LAICI

Dryden was a member of the Church of England in 1682, and this poem is a statement of his religious position. ' I pretend not ', he said in the Preface, ' to make myself a judge of faith in others, but only to make a confession of my own.' The transition from political satire was not so violent as it may seem now, for religion was at the root of the great political questions of the day ; and indeed this poem is permeated with politics. But Dryden's purpose was to make his position clear to himself. He thinks upon paper, and his thought becomes clearer as he proceeds. That he should choose such a subject would show that, though ' naturally inclined to scepticism in philosophy ' (Preface), he had begun to be troubled with religious doubts. The poem is a plea for the *via media* between submission to authority and individual independence. But it contains evidence that Dryden had not yet attained a final resting place.

PAGE **85**, l. 18.   *interfering*, striking against each other, colliding ; Latin *ferire*. Cf. ' jarring atoms ', p. 106, l. 4.

l. 21.   *the Stagirite*, Aristotle, born at Stageira in Thrace.

l. 28.   Cf. Prologue to *Aureng-zebe*, l. 10, p. 54.

l. 335.   *disinteressed*. Dryden regularly uses the form *interess* (cf. Fr. *intéresser*).

l. 346.   *provoke*, appeal (to a higher ecclesiastical tribunal).

l. 381.   *took . . . on content*, accepted without examination. Cf. Pope, *Essay on Criticism*, l. 308 : ' The Sense they humbly take upon content.'

l. 393.   *cheated on record*, by misrepresentation of the written record.

l. 453.   ' If any one be so lamentable a critic as to require the smoothness, the numbers, and the turn of heroic poetry in this poem, I must tell him that, if he has not read Horace, I have studied him, and hope the style of his Epistles is not ill imitated here. The expressions of a poem designed purely for instruction ought to be plain and natural, and yet majestic. . . . A man is to be cheated into passion, but to be reasoned into truth ' (Preface).

l. 454. Cf. Horace, *Satires*, I. iv. 42, ' sermoni propriora.'

l. 456. *Tom Sternhold* (d. 1549), who versified the Psalms along with John Hopkins.

TO THE MEMORY OF JOHN OLDHAM

John Oldham (1653–83) made his name by his *Satires upon the Jesuits*, written in 1679, when he was twenty-six. He was more than twenty years younger than Dryden, but he preceded Dryden as a satirist : hence l. 8.

PAGE **90,** l. 9. *Nisus.* See *Aeneid* v. 328.

ll. 13, 14. Dryden's own experience. He mastered the heroic couplet about the age of forty. See note on The Dramas.

l. 23. *Marcellus.* See *Aeneid* vi. 855, 883.

HORACE, ODE 29, BOOK III

' Pindaric verse ' gets its name from the Pindaric Odes of Cowley. Unlike the Odes of Pindar, which they professed to imitate only in style and manner, they were irregular in structure, the stanzas having no defined form and the verses no regular length.

In this translation Dryden does not attempt to reproduce the spirit of Horace's Ode. He makes the experiment of translating from the quieter manner of Horace into the vehement manner of Pindar that ' bears down all before it with impetuous force '.

Dryden's Pindarics date from 1685. In March he brought out his *Threnodia Augustalis : A Funeral-Pindarique Poem Sacred to the Happy Memory of King Charles II*.

TO THE MEMORY OF MRS. ANNE KILLIGREW

Anne Killigrew, maid of honour to Mary of Modena, Duchess of York and the Queen of James II, died of small-pox on 16 June 1685 at the age of twenty-five. Her poems fill a quarto volume of a hundred pages ; Dryden's great Ode is prefixed to them.

PAGE **94,** l. 23. *traduction.* The doctrine of traduction, or traducianism, maintained that the soul of man is transmitted from his parents, in opposition to the view that a new soul is created at birth.

l. 26. *Thy father*, the Rev. Henry Killigrew (1613–1700), who had published Latin verses, and a tragedy, *The Conspiracy*, 1638.

l. 43.   *in trine.*   Planets located in the zodiacal signs so as to be distant from one another by 120°, i. e. one *third* of the Zodiac, were said to be in trine, and their influence was held to be favourable.

l. 68.   The nymph Arethusa was pursued by Alpheus under land and sea to Sicily, where she was changed by Diana into the fountain bearing her name in the island of Ortygia off Syracuse.   Cf. *Lycidas*, l. 85.

l. 162.   *Orinda.*   Katherine Philips (1631–64), ' the matchless Orinda ', whose *Poems* were published in 1664 (surreptitiously) and 1667.   She too died of small-pox.

l. 165.   *her warlike brother.*   There were two brothers in the navy—Henry, admiral, d. 1712, and James, captain, killed in action 1695.

THE HIND AND THE PANTHER

Dryden joined the Roman Church towards the beginning of 1686.   *The Hind and the Panther* appeared in April 1687. It is his longest original poem.

Like the *Religio Laici* it is a statement of his faith, but whereas in that poem he feels his way to a reasoned acceptance of Anglicanism, in *The Hind and the Panther* he writes with conviction of the truth of his new religion, and in the hope of seeing the Anglicans reconciled to it.   The Church of England, the Panther, is the ' noblest ' form of Protestantism ; as hitherto, the height of Dryden's scorn is reserved for the Nonconformists.

Dryden has often been said to have changed his religion in the hope of bettering his position under a Roman Catholic king, and payments that he received as laureate have been cited in proof.   But see E. K. Broadus, *The Laureateship, A Study of the Office of Poet Laureate in England*, 1921, pp. 59–74, where the facts are for the first time stated satisfactorily ; and cf. p. 201, note on p. 154, l. 7.   The fervour of the quoted passages on Belief and Conversion speaks to their sincerity ; and to the end of his life Dryden never faltered in his new faith.

PAGE **100.**   *Belief.*   ' These lines are of great autobiographical importance.   They help to explain Dryden's conversion to Roman Catholicism.   In his manhood he followed "false lights", i. e. the fashionable scepticism of the period, based on the theories of Hobbes.   What attracted him to the Roman Church was the conviction of the fallibility of his own judgement, and the desire "for an unerring guide" ' (C. H. Firth).

ll. 32–6.   Quoted by Gibbon in his *Autobiography*, when describing his conversion to Roman Catholicism in his ' impetuous ' youth.

PAGE **102.**   *The Fable of the Swallows.*   This describes the prosperity of the Roman Catholics under James II, and predicts their misfortunes. The swallows vote a flight as winter is coming, but the younger birds hesitate and are supported by the martin (which migrates the latest of the swallow tribe), and the flight is delayed till all are overtaken by bad weather. The details of the fable have historical significance—the martin, for instance, is Father Petre, James II's confessor (for other points see Scott's note in his edition of Dryden, vol. x) ; but, as Hazlitt said of *The Faerie Queene*, if we do not meddle with the allegory it will not meddle with us. Dryden speaks of this fable in his Preface as 'a distinct story by itself'. It anticipates his volume of *Fables*. In addition to its merits as vivid, rapid narrative, it shows Dryden at his best in natural description.

l. 12. Cf. Horace, *Satires*, I. i. 36, ' simul inversum contristat Aquarius annum '. Cf. p. 198, note on song, p. 141, l. 4.

l. 30. *mackrel gale*. The best time for catching mackerel is when a fresh breeze is blowing.

l. 74. The sun passes from the Virgin (*Virgo*) and enters the Balance (*Libra*) on 21 September. The collocation ' Virgin Balance ' is awkward, but means the Balance. Virgo was identified with Astræa, the goddess of justice, and the Balance was the scales of justice. The sun enters Capricorn on 21 December.

l. 85. *dorp*, village ; a Dutch word, English *thorpe*.

l. 88. *Sick-feathered*, with young, weak feathers, used especially of birds in moulting time. Cf. Keats, *Eve of St. Agnes*, xxxvii, ' A dove . . . with sick unpruned wing.'

l. 105. *poled them down*, struck them down with poles.

ll. 109–12. It was generally understood to be the king-fisher which ' hanged by the bill, sheweth in what quarter the wind is by an occult and secret propriety ' : see Sir Thomas Browne, *Vulgar Errors*, III. x. But Browne mentions the view that it should be hung by the back ' that by the bill it might point out the quarters of the wind, for so hath Kircherus described the Orbis and the Sea Swallow '.

SONG FOR ST. CECILIA'S DAY

A series of annual celebrations of St. Cecilia, the patron saint of music, had been instituted by 1683, in which year the music was written by Henry Purcell. For an account of the celebrations see Malone, *Prose Works of Dryden*, 1800, i, pp. 254–307, and W. H. Husk, *Celebrations on St. Cecilia's Day*, 1857.

Dryden wrote the words for the celebrations in 1687 and 1697. It is important to remember that his *Song for St. Cecilia's Day* and *Alexander's Feast* were written to be set to music.

' The essential merit of Dryden's poem is that he has seized the principle that variations of rhythm, if not echoed and repeated—as they are in a poem composed of stanzas—can have value only so far as they illustrate the sense ; otherwise they are mere licences. This principle is not only grasped but, by the peculiar felicity of the occasion, it is perfectly realized ; the theme, the power of music, allows the illustrations of sense by rhythm to be everywhere explicit ' (A. W. Verrall, *Lectures on Dryden*, 1914, p. 194).

PAGE **106**, l. 15. *diapason* (Greek διὰ πασῶν (τῶν χορδῶν), through all the strings), the whole range of notes in the scale.

l. 17. *Jubal*, ' the father of all such as handle the harp and organ ', *Genesis* iv. 21.

l. 52. Cecilia is honoured as the inventress of the organ, but ' the pneumatic organ is said to have been of still higher antiquity than this pious lady ' (Malone), and when her name came to be associated with the organ is not known. In the *Golden Legend* it is her piety that drew an angel down from heaven. She is supposed to have suffered martyrdom at the beginning of the third century.

TO MY DEAR FRIEND MR. CONGREVE

Dryden wrote poetical epistles or addresses throughout all his career, but the best of them belong to the last ten years of his life. Scott calls this epistle ' one of the most elegant and apparently heartfelt effusions of friendship that our language boasts '. In addition to its personal interest, it is a valuable critical document.

The Double Dealer was acted in November 1693 and published in December (but dated 1694). It was Congreve's second play, and was not so successful on the stage as his first, *The Old Bachelor*. In a letter to William Walsh, 12 December 1693, Dryden wrote : ' His *Double Dealer* is much censured by the greater part of the Town : and is defended only by the best judges, who, you know, are commonly the fewest, yet it gets ground daily. . . . My verses which you will find before it were written before the play was acted, but I neither altered them nor do I alter my opinion of the play.' Congreve was then a young man of only twenty-three. Dryden was always generous in his encouragement of youthful talent. He recognized at once that Congreve was his superior in comedy.

PAGE **110**, l. 7. *Janus* in classical fable introduced agriculture and civilization into ancient Italy.

l. 15. *Vitruvius*, Roman architect of the time of Julius Caesar and Augustus, author of the only ancient treatise on architecture that has come down to us.

l. 29. *courtship*, courtliness.

ll. 39, 40. An error : Giulio Romano (1492–1546) was nine years younger than Raphael (1483–1520) and from the first was Raphael's pupil. Dryden would seem to have confused him with Pietro Perugino (1446–1524).

l. 41. Dryden lost the offices of Poet Laureate and Historiographer Royal at the Revolution, and was succeeded in both by Thomas Shadwell (' Tom the First '). On Shadwell's death in 1692, Nahum Tate was appointed Laureate, and Thomas Rymer (' Tom the Second ') was appointed Historiographer. As the plural number of the next line shows, Tate is included under the designation suggested by Rymer's name. Cf. *The Dunciad* i. 6, ' Still Dunce the second reigns like Dunce the first '.

Rymer merited his office ; his *Foedera* is invaluable to the historian. But he also wrote bad, if learned, criticism (his *Short View of Tragedy*, 1693, in which he attacks Shakespeare, had just appeared), and he had written a bad play, *Edgar*, in illustration of his own idea of a good tragedy ; and Dryden has these in mind. Cf. his reference to Rymer in the Prologue to *Love Triumphant*, 1694 :

> To Shakespeare's critic he bequeaths the curse,
> To find his faults, and yet himself make worse ;
> A precious reader in poetic schools,
> Who by his own examples damns his rules.

l. 49. *my patron*, the Earl of Dorset, who as Lord Chamberlain (1689–97) appointed to the offices of Poet Laureate and Historiographer. He helped Dryden privately when for religious reasons he could not recognize him officially. Dryden thereupon dedicated his translation of Juvenal to Dorset (1693) and made public acknowledgement of Dorset's ' action of pure disinterested charity '. The passage is given on p. 154 ; it ought to be read in connexion with this couplet.

Dorset is the Eugenius of the essay *Of Dramatic Poesy* : see p. 143, l. 18 note.

l. 63. *she*, clearly an oversight ; in l. 69, *his*. In all probability Dryden had written ' Nature had once was prodigal before ' (cf. ' Nature ' in the lines on Milton, p. 108), but, on noticing that he had just used ' native ', hastily altered ' Nature ' to ' Heaven ' (a monosyllable) and inserted ' but ' for the sake of the metre.

l. 72. Congreve brought out an edition of Dryden's plays : see the note on the Dedication, pp. 1–3.

ALEXANDER'S FEAST

See the note on the *Song for St. Cecilia's Day*, 1687. In a letter to his sons at Rome Dryden wrote on 3 September 1697 : ' I am writing a song for St. Cecilia's Feast, who, you know, is the patroness of music. This is troublesome, and no way beneficial ; but I could not deny the stewards of the feast, who came in a body to me to desire that kindness '. This passage disposes of the story that Dryden sat up a whole night writing it and finished it ' at one sitting ' (J. Warton, *Essay on Pope*, 1782, ii. 20, 21), or at least shows that it must not be taken literally. But Dryden wrote with great rapidity once he caught fire, and the Ode has the unity of unbroken composition. Johnson understood that Dryden spent a fortnight in writing and correcting it.

The subject of the poem is taken from a passage in Plutarch's life of Alexander : When Alexander was at Persepolis ' he diverted himself with his officers at an entertainment of drinking, and other pastimes, and indulged so far as to have every one his mistress sit by and drink with them. The most celebrated of them was Thais an Athenian, Ptolemy's mistress, who was afterwards king of Egypt '. She flattered Alexander, and then, in affection for her country, proposed to set fire to the palace of Xerxes, who had reduced the city of Athens to ashes. ' What she said was received with such universal liking and murmurs of applause, and so seconded by the encouragement and eagerness of the company, that the King himself, persuaded to be of the party, started from his seat, and with a chaplet of flowers on his head, and a lighted torch in his hand, led the way.' The quotations are from the translation of Plutarch to which Dryden contributed the introductory Life of Plutarch, 1683.

In December 1697 Dryden wrote to Jacob Tonson, his publisher : ' I am glad to hear from all hands that my Ode is esteemed the best of all my poetry, by all the town : I thought so myself when I writ it ; but, being old, I mistrusted my own judgment.' Its beauties were undisputed till the nineteenth century announced that they belonged rather to rhetoric than to poetry.

PAGE 113, l. 20. *Timotheus*, a musician of Thebes. The story of his playing before Alexander, and of Alexander's excitement, comes from Suidas (fl. A. D. 970), but the instrument of which Suidas speaks is not the lyre but the flute.

l. 25. Cf. Virgil, *Eclogues*, iii. 60 : ' ab Iove principium musae '. Alexander was reputed to be the son of Jove, who was said to have assumed the form of a serpent or dragon about the time when Olympias, his mother, was married to Philip of Macedon.

l. 34. *admire*, wonder at.

l. 41. Cf. *Aeneid* x. 115 : ' adnuit et totum nutu tremefecit Olympum '.

l. 69. *The master*, Timotheus.

ll. 75, 79. *good—blood*, a perfect rhyme in the seventeenth century. Note that *fallen*, l. 77, does not rhyme.

l. 95. *'Twas but*, &c., a kindred sound had only to be moved. The idiom is French rather than English (il n'y avait qu'à).

l. 97. Cf. *L'Allegro*, l. 136 : ' in soft Lydian airs '.

l. 127. *horrid*, rough, rude ; Lat. *horridus*.

l. 162. *the vocal frame*, the organ.

l. 163. *enthusiast*, one divinely inspired.

ll. 169, 170. See note on *Song for St. Cecilia's Day* 1687, l. 52 ; and Johnson's criticism, p. 18, ll. 24–9.

CYMON AND IPHIGENIA

For the origin and growth of Dryden's *Fables*, see the Preface, pp. 160–80. Dryden began by translating Homer and Ovid, then translated Chaucer ' into our language as it is now refined ', not in the hope of improving him but in order that he might ' perpetuate his memory ', then imitated Chaucer by taking stories from Boccaccio's *Decameron* and making them the subjects of original poems. *Cymon and Iphigenia* is based on *Decameron*, Fifth day, Novel 1. *Boccace* is the English form of Boccaccio, and was regularly used till the nineteenth century.

In his three tales from Boccaccio (*Sigismonda and Guiscardo, Theodore and Honoria*, and *Cymon and Iphigenia*) Dryden shows himself a master of the short story in verse. Wordsworth thought that they were ' the best, at least the most poetical, of his poems ' (Letter to Scott, 7 November 1805).

PAGE **120,** l. 48. *sincere*, without alloy : cf. *Absalom and Achitophel*, l. 43.

l. 179. *cudden*, fool, dolt.

l. 237. *of the better hand*, of the better sort, tendency ; on the right side. Cf. Dryden, *Defence of an Essay of Dramatic Poesy*, 1668 (*Essays*, ed. W. P. Ker, i. 118), ' I have committed an error on the right hand, by commending too much the copiousness and well-sounding of our language ' ; and his translation of Persius, 1693, Satire VI, Argument, ' One error, though on the right hand, yet a great one, is . . . '

l. 337. *prevents*, is too quick for, forestalls.

l. 341. *different*, carrying in opposite directions.

l. 396. The semicolon must be retained after *fear*, which is intransitive and balances *exults* ; but *fear* is understood to be used transitively before *Not them but theirs*, i. e. not *the vanquished side* but their countrymen, whose numbers deprived the victors of the chance of flight.

l. 400. ' Dryden willingly seizes the opportunity of being witty at the expense of the militia of England, which were then drawn out, and exercised once a month, instead of being formed as at present into permanent fencible regiments ; differing from those of the line only in the mode of raising them, and the extent of service ' (Scott—during the Napoleonic wars).

l. 424. *the church of womankind,* alluding to the doctrine of passive obedience.

l. 427. *It rested,* &c., it remained either to drop Cymon or to raise him up again.

l. 429. *pleased,* was determined ; Latin *placuit.* Cf. l. 557.

l. 484. *menage,* a variant of *manage,* common in Dryden's time, and used in the sense of French *ménager,* to husband, treat carefully.

l. 539. *provoke,* call forth, summon ; Latin *provocare.* For another sense, see *Religio Laici,* l. 346.

l. 552. *suborn,* prepare, provide ; Latin *subornare.*

l. 557. *It pleased.* Cf. l. 429.

l. 559. *required,* demanded.

l. 608. *floats,* overspreads, drenches, inundates.

l. 613. *buxom,* pliant, yielding. Cf. ' the buxom air ', *Faerie Queene* I. xi. 37 and *Paradise Lost* II. 842.

l. 624. *missive,* missile ; regular in the seventeenth century.

SONGS AND LYRICAL PASSAGES

These passages exhibit the variety of measures to be found in Dryden's lyrics. He is not one of our great song writers because in his songs he is habitually playful and hasty, and only occasionally (as in the passage from *Cleomenes*) does he express deep and poignant feeling ; but in the technique of his verse he is a master, without a rival in his time or for long after.

PAGE **139.** *Farewell ungrateful traitor.* The verse is copied by Keats in his song ' In a drear-nighted December '.

l. 3. *creature,* commonly pronounced at this time *cray-tur.*

PAGE **141.** *Ask not the cause.* ' A splendid example of its style ' (Saintsbury).

l. 4. Cf. p. 193, note on *The Hind and the Panther,* p. 102, l. 12.

PAGE **142.** *The Secular Masque* was written by Dryden for his benefit performance at Drury Lane on 25 March 1700. The day chosen in honour of the old poet was supposed to be the first day of the new century. Up to 1752 the official year began not on 1 January but on 25 March ; and 1700 was wrongly taken by the theatre managers to be the first year of the new century, not the last of the old.

The subject of the masque, as the title shows, was the century which was supposed to have ended. ' By the introduction of the deities of the chase, of war, and of love, as governing the various changes of the seventeenth century, the poet alludes to the sylvan sports of James I, the bloody wars of his son, and the licentious gallantry which reigned in the courts of Charles II and James his successor ' (Scott). The whole piece is written with great spirit, and is of great interest prosodically. Only the closing lines are here given. They were probably the last that Dryden wrote.

OF DRAMATIC POESY

This Essay was written ' in the country ', probably at Charlton in Wiltshire, while the theatres were shut on account of the Plague (May 1665 to Christmas 1666), but parts of it belong to 1667. It was published late in 1667, though dated 1668. It was Dryden's only critical work that was issued by itself ; his other essays were Prefaces.

The introduction passes brilliantly from the battle of 3 June 1665 to contemporary poetry, and ends with a statement of Dryden's aims in verse. The second extract is Dryden's famous estimate of the great Elizabethans.

The text is from the revised edition of 1684.

PAGE **143**, l. 1. *that memorable day*, 3 June 1665. The English fleet was commanded by the Duke of York.

l. 15. *the park*, St. James's Park.

l. 18. *Eugenius*, Charles Sackville, Lord Buckhurst, afterwards Sixth Earl of Dorset ; see note on ' my patron ', *Epistle to Congreve*, p. 111, l. 49.

Crites, Sir Robert Howard (1626–98), son of the Earl of Berkshire, and the brother of Dryden's wife. Dryden had collaborated with him in *The Indian Queen*.

Lisideius, Sir Charles Sedley (1639–1701), best known now for his lyrics. His ' borrowed name ' is an anagram of the Latin form *Sidleius*.

Neander, Dryden.

l. 25. *the bridge*, London Bridge, then the only bridge.

PAGE **144**, l. 15. *congratulated to the rest that*, now ' congratulated the rest on that ' ; a regular usage in Dryden's time.

l. 22. *concernment*, importance.

PAGE **145**, l. 17. *Quem in concione*, &c. Cicero, *Pro Archia* x.

l. 29. *one of them*, Robert Wild (1609–79), a dissenting clergyman, whose ' famous poem ' (p. 147, l. 9) was *Iter Boreale*, ' attempting something upon the successful and matchless march of the Lord General George Monk from Scotland to London, in the winter 1659 ', published 1660. He at once brought out *An Essay upon the late victory obtained by the Duke of York upon June 3, 1665* (licensed 16 June), some time before Dryden wrote this passage. Dryden had presumably seen the poem when he expressed his ' mortal apprehension '.

l. 30. *clenches*, or ' clinches ', puns, plays upon words.

l. 31. *catachresis*, ' an improper kind of speech, . . . the expressing of one matter by the name of another which is incompatible with, and sometimes clean contrary to it ' (*The Mysterie of Rhetorique unvail'd*, by John Smith, 1657, p. 48).

l. 32. *Clevelandism.* John Cleveland (1613–58) was the most vigorous of the Cavalier satirical poets. In a later section of this Essay, Dryden says ' we cannot read a verse of Cleveland's without making a face at it, as if every word were a pill to swallow : he gives us many times a hard nut to break our teeth, without a kernel for our pains '.

PAGE **146,** l. 7. *my other extremity of poetry*, unidentified ; Richard Flecknoe (see note on *MacFlecknoe*) has been suggested. He wrote verses on the victory, which were included in his *Epigrams* in 1670.

l. 15. *ten little words.* Cf. Pope, *Essay on Criticism*, ll. 346, 347 :

> While expletives their feeble aid do join,
> And ten low words oft creep in one dull line.

l. 23. *Pauper*, &c. Martial, *Epigrams* viii. 19.

PAGE **147,** l. 6. *Withers*, i. e. George Wither (1588–1667). His later work overshadowed the delicacy of his early poems, to which justice was not done till the nineteenth century. Cf. *The Dunciad* I. 296.

l. 12. *by the candles' ends*, a method of auction adopted from France ; bids were accepted while the candle-end kept burning.

l. 19. *Qui Bavium*, &c. Virgil, *Eclogues* iii. 90 (' Who hates not Bavius, let him love thy songs ').

l. 28. *Petronius, Satyricon* ii.

PAGE **148,** l. 8. *Indignor*, &c. Horace, *Epistles* II. i. 76, 77. (' I lose my patience, and I own it too, When works are censured not as bad but new.' Pope.)

l. 11. *Si meliora*, &c. Ibid. 34, 35 (' If Time improve our wit as well as wine, Say at what age a Poet grows divine.' Pope.)

PAGE **150,** ll. 7–34. See Johnson on this ' model of encomiastic criticism ', p. 4, ll. 20 et seq.

l. 24. *Quantum*, &c. Virgil, *Eclogues* i. 25.

l. 25. *Mr. Hales,*—John Hales (1584–1656), fellow of Eton. *The Golden Remains of the Ever Memorable Mr. John Hales* was published in 1659. The same anecdote is given in Charles Gildon's *Reflections on Mr. Rymer's Short View of Tragedy*, 1694, and in Nicholas Rowe's *Life of Shakespeare*, 1709, with additional details which date it 1633–7.

PAGE **151,** l. 4. *while he lived.* Beaumont died in 1616. There is no evidence that Jonson submitted his plays to Beaumont's censure. For ' the verses he writ to him ', see Jonson, *Epigrams* 55 : ' How do I love thee, Beaumont, and thy Muse '.

DISCOURSE ON SATIRE

This Discourse is the Dedication (to the Earl of Dorset) of Dryden's translation of Juvenal and Persius. It illustrates Dryden's statement that ' the nature of a preface is rambling ' (p. 168, l. 27), and contains several passages which may be removed without loss from their setting. In the passages here given Dryden speaks of himself or his writings.

PAGE **153**, l. 11. *King Arthur*. This passage suggested to Scott the lines in *Marmion* (Canto I, Introduction) beginning

> And Dryden, in immortal strain,
> Had raised the Table Round again.

PAGE **154**, l. 3. *machines*, the supernatural agencies in a heroic poem, whether the gods and goddesses of classical mythology, or the Godhead and angels of the Christian religion. Dryden had argued that ' Christian poets have not hitherto been acquainted with their own strength '.

l. 7. *my little salary ill paid*. Dryden's salary on his appointment as Poet Laureate and Historiographer was £200 with ' one butt or Pype of the best Canary Wyne '. In 1679 his salary was raised to £200 as Historiographer and £100 as Laureate, with the butt of wine. But the salary was never paid punctually ; there is a Treasury warrant of 6 May 1684 for the payment of arrears since 1680. See E. K. Broadus, *The Laureateship*, 1921, pp. 61–3.

l. 13. *your charity*. See notes on p. 111, l. 49 and p. 143, l. 18.

PAGE **157**, l. 24. *Heinsius*,—Daniel Heinsius (1580–1655), Dutch scholar, in his *De Satyra Horatiana*, ed. 1629, pp. 50 et seq. Heinsius is quoted by Barten Holyday : see l. 16.

l. 31. *secuit*, &c. Persius, *Sat*. i. 114.

PAGE **158**, l. 1. *Ense*, &c. Juvenal, *Sat*. i. 165.

l. 4. *Holyday*,—Barten Holyday (1593–1661), sometime Archdeacon of Oxford ; his translation of Persius appeared in 1616, and his Juvenal posthumously in 1673. Dryden quotes from the Preface to the Juvenal : ' Juvenal's change of the ancient Satyre was, methinks, not only a Change, but a Perfection. For, what is the end of Satyre, but to Reform ? whereas a perpetual Grin does rather Anger than Mend '. Dryden had Holyday's preface lying open before him, and took several points from it.

l. 17. *Stapylton*, Sir Robert (d. 1669), published *The First Six Satyrs* of Juvenal in English verse in 1644, and a complete version in 1647.

PAGE **159**, l. 18. *Jack Ketch* (d. 1686), public executioner, notorious for his barbarity : see Macaulay's *History*, ch. v (execution of Monmouth).

l. 22. *Zimri*. See *Absalom and Achitophel*, ll. 544–68.

Buckingham ' began the frolic ' by satirizing Dryden in *The Rehearsal*.

l. 31. *obnoxious*, liable, exposed ; the usual sense in the seventeenth century.

PREFACE TO FABLES

This was the last of Dryden's critical essays, and of itself is sufficient to explain Dryden's belief that ' what judgment I had increases rather than diminishes '. It contains our first great estimate of Chaucer, which ranks with the estimate of Shakespeare in his early essay *Of Dramatic Poesy*. It is memorable also for what it tells us about Dryden himself.

PAGE **160,** l. 9. *a certain nobleman*, the Duke of Buckingham —Zimri. The palace is Cliveden.

PAGE **161,** l. 3. *Sandys*, George (1578–1644), translator of Ovid's *Metamorphoses*, 1621–6.

l. 11. *Spenser.* See *The Faerie Queene*, IV. ii. 34.

l. 17. Fairfax's translation of Tasso, *Godfrey of Bulloigne, or the Recovery of Jerusalem*, was published in 1600.

l. 32. Chaucer was supposed, by reason of his court connexions, to have been Poet Laureate, but the office was not definitely established till the seventeenth century. See E. K. Broadus, *The Laureateship*, p. 16.

PAGE **162,** l. 11. *octave rhyme.* This stanza was used before Boccaccio, but he established it as the ' measure for heroic verse '.

l. 24. *Rymer.* See note (p. 195) on epistle *To Mr. Congreve*, l. 41 (p. 111) ; here Dryden properly commends Rymer's learning. Rymer's account of Chaucer's debt to Provençal is to be found in his *Short View of Tragedy*, 1693, pp. 77, 78. Dryden does not distinguish between Provençal and Old French.

PAGE **164,** l. 8. *staved*, broken up into staves, like contraband hogsheads.

l. 21. *Horace,—Ars Poetica*, l. 322.

l. 23. *right in court*, a translation of the legal phrase *rectus in curia*, said of a man who has put himself right by getting rid of some disability which might have been brought up against him in court, e. g. by having a sentence of outlawry reversed.

l. 27. *a religious lawyer*, Jeremy Collier, in his *Short View of the Immorality and Profaneness of the English Stage*, 1698.

PAGE **165,** l. 31. *philology*, the study of literature, polite learning.

PAGE **166,** ll. 5, 6. There is no certain direct borrowing from the *Decameron* in the *Canterbury Tales*.

l. 9. *the invention of Petrarch.* Dryden has got the facts

wrong.   Petrarch translated into Latin the story of Griselda
as told by Boccaccio in the *Decameron* (last story).

l. 11.   *a Lombard author.*   Chaucer calls him ' Lollius ' : see
Skeat's *Chaucer*, ii, p. liii.   But Boccaccio is the main source.

l. 27.   *The Cock and the Fox* is not Chaucer's own in outline.
The main element in the story had been told by Marie de
France, and there is evidence that Chaucer was acquainted
with a more developed French version.

PAGE **167,** l. 29.   *inopem me copia fecit,* Ovid, *Metamorphoses,* iii. 466.

l. 33.   *John Littlewit,* at the beginning of Ben Jonson's
Bartholomew Fair : ' A pretty conceit, and worth the finding.
I have such luck to spin out these fine things still, and,
like a silk-worm, out of myself. . . . There I am again ! I do
feel conceits coming upon me, more than I am able to turn
tongue to.'

PAGE **169,** l. 5.   *One of our late great poets,* Cowley.   Cf.
Dryden's *Discourse on Satire (Essays,* ed. W. P. Ker, ii, p. 108) :
' I looked over the darling of my youth, the famous Cowley ;
there I found . . . the points of wit, the quirks of epigram, even
in the *Davideis,* an heroic poem, which is of an opposite nature
to those puerilities.'

l. 24.   *Catullus,* a mistake for *Martial,*—iii. 44 : ' Quid sit
scire cupis : nimis poeta es.'

l. 27.   *Tacitus,—De Oratoribus,* xxi : ' auribus judicum
accommodata '.

l. 34.   *he who published the last edition of him,* Thomas
Speght, whose two editions of Chaucer were published in 1598
and 1602, the latter being reprinted in 1687.   The accuracy of
Chaucer's versification has been undisputed since Tyrwhitt's
edition of the *Canterbury Tales,* 1775–8 ; but in Dryden's
defence it must be noted that he knew Chaucer only in a
corrupt text.   At the conclusion of his volume of *Fables* he
printed the texts which he had modernized, and they abound
in verses ' which are lame for want of half a foot ' : e. g.

> Whylom, as old Stories tellen us,
> There was a Duke that hight *Theseus* . . .
> That greater was non under the Son.

Dryden could not scan these lines as they stand.   Had he
known Chaucer in a good text, it is doubtful if he would have
written his versions.

PAGE **170,** l. 16.   *Harington.*   Sir John Harington's translation of Ariosto, *Orlando Furioso in English Heroical Verse,*
appeared in 1591.

l. 27.   *Baptista Porta* (1538–1615), the famous Italian
physiognomist, author of *De Humana Physiognomonia,* 1591.

PAGE **171,** l. 6. *gap-toothed,* Prologue to *Canterbury Tales,* l. 468, where modern editions read *gat-toothed.*

l. 9. *choice,* perhaps a misprint for *chace.*

PAGE **172,** ll. 5 et seq.   Prologue to *Canterbury Tales,* ll. 725–42. On the faults of the text, see note on p. 169, l. 34.
ll. 36, 37. The Miller's Tale, ll. 77, 78.

PAGE **173,** l. 6. *the late Earl of Leicester,* Philip Sidney, third Earl (1619–98), brother of Algernon Sidney.   Dryden dedicated *Don Sebastian* to him, 1690.

PAGE **174,** ll. 10–12. *Knight's Tale,* ll. 1204–6.

l. 16. *Milbourne,* Luke (1649–1720), who brought out *Notes on Dryden's Virgil,* 1698, a sustained attack of over two hundred pages.

PAGE **175,** l. 3. *Multa,* &c. Horace, *Ars Poetica,* 70–2.

l. 23. *some old Saxon friends,* friends who knew ' old Saxon ', i. e. Anglo-Saxon and the older forms of English. Great progress was being made in Anglo-Saxon studies at this time at Oxford, under the direction of George Hickes, Edmund Gibson, Christopher Rawlinson, Edward Thwaites, Thomas Benson, Humphrey Wanley, and others.   Perhaps Dryden was thinking also of Rymer, who deals briefly with ' British, Saxon, Norman, Latin, and Provençal ' poetry in England in his *Short View of Tragedy.*

PAGE **176,** l. 1. *grandam gold,* hoarded wealth : cf. Dryden, *The Wild Gallant,* 1663, iv. 1 : ' now I think on't, Frances has one hundred and twenty pieces of old grandam-and-aunt gold left her '.   Cf. also the Latin use of *anus,* as in ' testa vocatur anus ', Martial i. cvi. 4.

ll. 15–19. Nothing more is known of this translation by Mademoiselle de Scudéry, who died in June 1701 at the age of ninety-four.   By ' old Provençal ' Dryden again means old French ; cf. p. 162, l. 25.

PRINTED IN
GREAT BRITAIN
AT THE
UNIVERSITY PRESS
OXFORD
BY
CHARLES BATEY
PRINTER
TO THE
UNIVERSITY